*Poetic Statement
and Critical Dogma*

GERALD GRAFF

Poetic Statement and Critical Dogma

THE UNIVERSITY OF CHICAGO PRESS
CHICAGO AND LONDON

*To the memory
of my father*

The University of Chicago Press, Chicago 60637
The University of Chicago Press, Ltd., London

© 1970, 1980 by Gerald Graff
All rights reserved. Published 1970
Paperback edition 1980
Printed in the United States of America
84 83 82 81 80   5 4 3 2 1

ISBN: 0–226–30601–1
LCN: 80–14318

*Permission has been granted by the publishers to quote
from the following works:*

"The Course of a Particular," from *Opus Posthumous* by Wallace
Stevens. Published in New York by Alfred A. Knopf, Inc., 1957, and
in London by Faber and Faber, Ltd., 1959. "Hillcrest," from *Collected
Poems* by Edwin Arlington Robinson. Copyright 1916, Edwin Arlington
Robinson, renewed 1944 by Ruth Nivison. Reprinted with permission of
The Macmillan Company. "Little Gidding," by T. S. Eliot. Published in
The Complete Poems and Plays, 1909–1950, New York: Harcourt, Brace
& World, Inc., 1950, and in *Four Quartets*, London: Faber and Faber,
Ltd., 1960. "Fall Wind," from *Traveling Through the Dark* by William
Stafford, Harper & Row, 1962. The poem originally appeared in *North-
west* (Winter, 1960–61) and is reprinted by permission of Harper & Row,
Publishers. "Canto LXXIV" and "Canto LXXI" from *The Cantos* by
Ezra Pound. Copyright 1948 by Ezra Pound. Reprinted by permission of
New Directions Publishing Corp. "Of Modern Poetry," from *The Col-
lected Poems of Wallace Stevens*, Alfred A. Knopf, Inc., 1954. *Poetry
and Opinion* by Archibald MacLeish, University of Illinois Press, 1950.

Contents

Preface to the Paperback Edition

Ever since Plato branded poets a pack of liars, the question of how literary works "mean" and what sort of truth-to-reality, if any, is to be attributed to their meanings has been a central preoccupation of literary theorists. In recent years, however, this "problem of belief" has had to share center stage with another problem, "the problem of the text." To venture a simplification, we can say that whereas critics had previously debated whether literary texts could tell the truth about the world, they now have come to debate whether literary criticism can tell the truth about literary texts. Nevertheless, as the present book suggests, these two problems—the referentiality and the determinacy of literary meanings—are closely related. And though the literary theorizing of the past decade has moved a considerable distance from the positions and concerns of the critics taken up in this book, problems like that of the nature of literary meaning and truth remain as pertinent today as ever. In fact, with respect to this particular problem, one could make the case that the more things have changed, the more they have stayed the same.

That resistance to viewing poetry as a mode of propositional statement, which I described in 1970, has, if anything, been intensified by application of structuralism, deconstruction, and speech-act theory. Of course, to deny that literature is propositional is not necessarily to embrace art for art's sake. The "New Critics" and others discussed below rejected *propositional* conceptions of poetry (and by extension, literature); yet most of them still insisted that poetry and literature are in some important way *referential*, that they yield important forms of knowledge and truth about the world. These critics sought to redefine, rather than eliminate, the connection between literature and external reality. By contrast, our newer critics, encouraged perhaps by recent experiments in "self-reflexive" fiction, challenge the very legitimacy of the concepts of "referentiality" and "external reality." Yet it remains an open question whether these new formalisms break with earlier ideas or merely push them to a logical extreme.

Not many assertions in Jonathan Culler's *Structuralist Poetics* (1975) would cause a reader to mistake its author for a New Critic. But two such assertions occur when Culler observes that, according to structuralism, "literature is something other than a statement about the world," and that it discourages "the unseemly rush from word to world" (p. 130). At the same time, Culler's account of structuralist poetics actually undermines this antithesis between statement and literature. Consider his "rule of significance," which he advances as a "primary convention" of reading a work *as literature*. According to this, we read a poem "as expressing a significant attitude to some problem concerning man and/or his relation to the universe" (p. 115). That is to say, a necessary (though not a sufficient) condition for experiencing a text as literature is that we attribute general significance to what happens in it. This convention, as Culler shows, permits us to transform virtually any piece of writing into literature (though not necessarily very good literature) by looking at it in a certain way, attributing an exemplary meaning to it. Presented in the right format (e.g., in a book of verse) the instructions on a box of laundry soap can be read as literature— perhaps as an ironic statement of the banality of modern life. But then, if reading a text as literary involves seeing it as an allegorical comment on problems concerning man and his relation to the universe, to call literature "something other than a statement about the world" seems inaccurate. Something *more*, yes; but something *other*, no. To say that literature expresses a "significant attitude" looks rather like a euphemistic way of saying that literature makes statements or assertions.

But how, finally, can one *know* whether literary works make genuine assertions, or only appear to make them? Theoretical debates about this problem frequently misfire, because the various parties fail to determine what *kind* of question they are arguing about and what types of evidence they would accept as relevant to an answer. Formalists argue that literature may "use" or "embody" ideas, but that if it actually asserts them it is propaganda and not literature. Moralists counter with George Orwell's argument that every writer "has a message, whether he admits it or not, and the minutest details of his work are influenced by it. All art is propaganda." On what basis can proponents of these logically incompatible positions try to justify their claims? As long as neither group poses the question of *how one knows* how to determine the status of apparent statement in literature, the quarrel fails to advance beyond assertion and counterassertion.

By suggesting that this kind of question can be restated as one about the conventions of reading, and thus about the behavior of actual readers, Culler usefully points us toward one means of resolving the stalemate. His discussion of the convention of significance suggests that readers naturalize literary works by "thematizing" them. We make sense of even the most complex, contradictory, and "decentered" works by organizing their contents in terms of significant propositions, and we take these propositions seriously as responses to such things as "man," and "his relation to the universe." Of course, we may need to distinguish between taking a proposition "seriously" and strictly believing it to be true (see below, pp. 151–60 and especially n. 12, p. 154). But in any case, we do not wholly suspend the question of credibility. Culler himself, when he discusses Flaubert's novels in *Flaubert: The Uses of Uncertainty*, takes Flaubert's world view more seriously than his distinction between literature and statement would permit. As John Reichert has pointed out, the presence of a genre "of poems that we read as statements seriously meant" is "corroborated by the way critics talk about poems when they are not burdened by the unnecessary precautions imposed by rigid theory."

Of course, the appeal to literary "convention" has to assume there is something about those texts on which we choose to invoke the convention that invites us to read them as literature. If we came upon the laundry-soap instructions in a book otherwise devoted to verse, we would assume that it was the author's purpose that we read them as literature, rather than as actual instructions. If readers naturalize literary texts by attributing to them significant attitudes to problems concerning man and/or his relation to the universe, this is finally because expressing such attitudes is one of the purposes of literary works.

This last point may appear to be contradicted by authors who deliberately construct their works to frustrate propositional readings, or even the attribution of referential "meaning," altogether. In William Gass's short novel *Willie Masters' Lonesome Wife*, for example, the reader is told explicitly that the words he reads are pure words (or pure concepts) and are not to be taken as referring to anything outside themselves. "These words are all I am," declares Gass's principal "character." "Believe me, pity me. Not even the Dane is any more than that." Gass has, evidently by fiat, forestalled what Culler calls "the unseemly rush from word to world." But has Gass actually succeeded in carrying out his purpose? One does not need to read far in this novella to see that it offers a number of assertions about the world in the very process of justifying its avoidance of assertions. Gass implies that the world of pure linguistic "concepts" is more orderly, satisfying, and proportioned than that real world with which literature is to have nothing to do. One misses the whole point of Gass's novella unless one organizes it around thematic statements about the disorderliness of reality and the superior orderliness of art. Granted, we would not want to confuse Gass's method with that of writers whose view of the world does not oblige them to try to avoid making assertions. But Gass has not liberated himself from assertions, even though it is his explicit purpose to do so—and this is fortunate for his work, for we would not take it seriously as literature if he had succeeded.

To take the world views in literary works as *asserted* seems so unavoidable that it may seem hard to account for the onslaught literary theorists have mounted against this practice. We can account for it partly by the pedagogical context of modern literary theory, the need to deal with students and lay readers often disposed to a crude "message hunting" approach to literature. Then, too, there is pressure exerted by the discipline of esthetics, a goal of which is to differentiate "art" from other forms of activity. The natural effect of this specialization is to devalue those aspects of art which it shares with nonartistic activity.

Finally, however, only larger cultural explanations can account for the vehemence with which the propositional view of literature has been rejected. One must examine the warfare of literary intellectuals against technology, commerce, and utilitarianism, and against the rational forms of discourse which have been discredited by their association with these things. As I try to show more extensively in *Literature against Itself: Literary Ideas in Modern Society* (Chicago, 1979), underlying the attacks on "statement," "objective truth," "logic," and "argument" as models for describing literary meaning is an indictment of the functional rationality of advanced industrial society, a rationality which reduces the rich complexity of experience to practical or commercial abstractions. I do not wholly reject this cultural criticism and I can certainly understand its motives. But the fact that certain social institutions specialize in reductive statements does not mean that all statements are reductive, any more than the fact that certain philistines have looked for messages in literature means that all messages are philistine. But if the propositional view of literature has come to be viewed as philistine, this is not very surprising, since few serious theorists have made any effort to rehabilitate it. This book tries to begin that effort.

Introduction

It is axiomatic for a large number of contemporary poetic theorists that a poem, as a poem, does not assert anything about the world. "It is never what a poem *says* which matters," writes I. A. Richards, "but what it *is*." "The greatest poets, as poets, . . . refrain from assertion."[1] "Literature," says Northrop Frye, "is a body of hypothetical thought and action: it makes, as literature, no statements or assertions."[2] The position is by no means restricted to noncognitivists like Richards or to advocates of theories of poetry as pure imagination like Frye. Writers like Cleanth Brooks, Allen Tate, and Philip Wheelwright, although claiming that poetry yields a significant kind of knowledge, nevertheless deny that poems may assert propositions about the external world or make truth claims in the manner of ordinary nonpoetic discourse. In our period, the customary starting point for theorizing about poetry is through its supposed radical opposition to discursive writing: the poem *is* experience, not mediated statement *about* experience; poetry gives no "truth of correspondence" concerning states of affairs outside the poem, for the poem is itself the object of the knowledge it contains and aspires only to "truth of coherence"; the

1. *Science and Poetry* (New York: W. W. Norton & Co., 1926), pp. 34–35; *Principles of Literary Criticism* (New York: Harcourt, Brace & World, 1928), p. 276.
2. *The Well-Tempered Critic* (Bloomington: Indiana University Press, 1963), p. 149.

poem is not an assertion of thought but a "dramatic enactment" or "presentation" of the process of thought. As T. S. Eliot puts it, the poet does not advocate certain beliefs but enacts *"what it feels like* to hold certain beliefs."[3]

One of the many recent handbook-anthologies modeled both in format and critical approach after *Understanding Poetry* by Brooks and Robert Penn Warren informs the student that "poetry does not demand our belief, it invites us to experience." Without pausing to explain just why poetry might not demand our belief *as well as* invite us to experience, the editors continue: "If we must ask a question, it should not be, 'Can I believe what this says?' but rather, 'Is it dramatically valid for the speaker of the poem to assert his belief in the way he does?' " "Poetry," the editors declare, "may best be read not as argument inviting us to debate nor as explanation inviting us to understand, but as drama inviting our involvement."[4] A second textbook encourages this antithesis of experience and understanding when it asserts that "the scientist communicates information; the poet experience."[5] Accordingly, the student must beware of regarding poems as if they asserted propositions. He must not attribute to Wordsworth's "Composed Upon Westminster Bridge" the statement, "the city is as beautiful a place to live in as the country," but he is on safe ground if he merely says that the poem deals with *"the natural beauty of the city."* For "the danger of regarding theme as message or moral decreases when a noun with appropriate

3. "The Social Function of Poetry," in *Critiques and Essays in Criticism, 1920–1948,* ed. R. W. Stallman (New York: Ronald Press Co., 1949), p. 107.

4. James E. Miller and Bernice Slote, eds., *The Dimensions of Poetry* (New York: Dodd, Mead & Co., 1966), pp. 101–2.

5. C. F. Main and Peter J. Seng, eds., *Poems* (Belmont, Calif.: Wadsworth Publishing Co., 1961), p. 52. See also another popular text, John Ciardi, *How Does a Poem Mean?* (Boston: Houghton Mifflin Co., 1959): "A poet must believe *something* passionately enough to have strong feelings about it, but what that *something* is in actual fact is the item of least consequence as far as participating in the poetic performance is concerned" (p. 769).

modifiers replaces the complete sentence."[6] By means of such grammatical circumspection, the student may presumably sterilize himself from the effects of reading a poem as if it had something to say.

This extreme divorce between the propositional and the "dramatic" is a common factor which runs through many otherwise diverse theories and underlies many recent metaphoric definitions of poetry: "language as gesture," "verbal icon," "symbolic action," "presentational symbol," "effigy," the play of conflicting tensions, impulses, paradoxes, ambiguities, etc. Such terms emphasize the presentational, dramatic character of poetry and separate poetry sharply from discursive statement. The term "dramatic," in fact, in the critical vocabulary of our period, has come to signify a uniquely antidiscursive semantic function, a capacity of language to operate in a way that has nothing to do with making assertions about reality.

The antithesis which has grown up between the propositional and the dramatic seems to me neither necessary nor desirable. Accordingly, the present study has a dual aim: first of all, to demonstrate the unfortunate theoretical and practical consequences of several types of antipropositional theories; and secondly to outline a poetics which finds a place for the propositional and assertive element in poetry and yet also does justice to the contemporary emphases upon organic unity and experiential complexity uniquely achieved in poetry.[7] Such a poetics would permit us to transcend the crippling either/or distinction between the propositional and the dramatic. The aim of the book is not to repudiate modern poetics in favor of an old-fashioned theory of statement but to define a common

6. Main and Seng, *Poems*, p. 66.

7. The term "antipropositional," which has been employed throughout the book, refers to theorists who deny that poetry asserts anything or makes propositional truth claims. Many of these theorists concede that poems may *contain* propositions, but they argue that these propositions should not be read as assertions.

meeting ground upon which the conflicting emphases of the old and the new—each incomplete in itself—may reach an accommodation and thus a mutual enrichment. Modern poetics is essentially a poetics of immediate *experience;* traditional, preromantic poetics is a poetics of the philosophic *understanding* of experience. In my view, these two aspects, the abstract, conceptual intelligence and the dramatic process of experience, cannot be seen as antithetical without enfeebling literature and criticism alike.

Although the book does not dwell on them, its argument contains implications regarding the current cultural plight of the humanities. Humanists frequently complain of the disproportionate prestige accorded to the sciences in the United States and of the "ruinous conflict," in Stuart N. Hampshire's phrase, between science and the humanities. What these same humanists do not seem to realize is that when they define the humanities, as Hampshire does, as an essentially private refuge of the emotions and desires from the everyday demands of objectivity and public reality, they do their part to widen and intensify the breach they deplore.[8] Those who deny objective truth claims to the arts, or who assert those truth claims only in the most hesitant, contradictory, and ambiguous terms, should not be shocked when others dismiss the arts as ornamental and inferior to the sciences. As Christopher Lasch has recently argued, the arts will not be raised from their "presently degraded, diffuse, and essentially ornamental position" in our universities and our culture until they are established "as studies that make their own indispensable contribution to the understanding of the objective world."[9]

A brief word concerning the sequence of chapters to follow may be helpful. The first four chapters consider the problem of poetic assertion and meaning as it has been treated by several

8. "A Ruinous Conflict," *Modern Writers and Other Essays* (New York: Alfred A. Knopf, 1970), pp. 194–95.

9. "Toward a New Program for the University," *TriQuarterly*, XVI (Fall, 1969), 203.

representative contemporary theorists, my purpose being to show that the tendency of these theorists to deny an assertive capacity to poetry invites numerous contradictions and confusions. The account begins by outlining the philosophical implications of organicist, antipropositional theories with respect to the main theoretical issues and proceeds in the next three chapters to an analysis of specific theories. Beginning with an unabashed noncognitivist theory—Richards' view of poetry as pseudo-statement—I proceed to examine the theories of mythopoeic critics and post-Ricardian New Critics, who make knowledge and truth claims for poetry. This classification raises difficulties, however, since the theories concerned frequently betray equivocation over the issue of the cognitive content of poetry: it is not always clear whether a given theory is cognitive or noncognitive, or, if it can be found to be cognitive, what is the content of the cognitions claimed. This equivocation is itself a symptom of the semantic confusions which in my opinion must beset any theorist who attempts to theorize about a kind of "meaning" which is not "about" anything or is "about itself." What is more, for reasons which will subsequently emerge, the apparent disagreement between the noncognitivism of Richards and the theories of such self-proclaimed cognitivists as Brooks is not so pronounced as may at first appear.

Chapter Five attempts to show that antipropositional theories —even insofar as the logical problems they encounter may be overlooked—fail to provide an adequate account of the concrete facts of poetic structure and meaning. Chapters Five and Six, although necessarily tentative and incomplete, argue the case that propositional assertion and expository argument are important semantic and structural principles of poetry, that "discourse," far from being alien to poetry, is a vital and necessary element which cannot be ignored in critical analysis.

I must point out that this study is circumscribed by a specific set of problems and does not claim to be a comprehensive survey of contemporary poetics. The criticisms of its chief subjects should not be taken to imply a condemnation of the total body of their theorizing. It has sometimes been convenient to group a number of very different critics together when they were in agreement upon a certain issue. This should not be taken to suggest that there are not radical differences between them in other respects.

The discussion of "poetry" in these pages is restricted specifically to the lyric poem, although the thesis has obvious implications with respect to literary works in general. The concentration upon the lyric is in conformity with the predominant emphasis of most of the critics with whom the book is concerned.

Poetic Statement
and Critical Dogma

CHAPTER ONE

Mythotherapy and Modern Poetics

A major problem encountered in the study of contemporary poetics is conveniently dramatized for us in John Barth's philosophical novel, *The End of the Road*.[1] The theme of this novel is that all interpretations of reality are arbitrary and are therefore equally valid or invalid. The chief character, Jacob Horner, repeatedly experiences an inability to decide which among the infinite number of possible hypotheses concerning the events of his life is the most likely, all hypotheses seeming equally plausible or implausible, and he consequently suffers from paralysis, both physical and psychological. There is simply no good reason for performing any act or making any choice or decision. For example, when it is suggested to him that he apply for a teaching position,

> Instantly a host of arguments against applying for a job at the Wicomico State Teachers College presented themselves for my use, and as instantly a corresponding number of

1. *The End of the Road*, rev. ed. (Garden City, N. Y.: Doubleday & Co., 1967).

refutations lined up opposite them, one for one, so that the question of my application was held static like the rope marker in a tug-o'-war where the opposing teams are perfectly matched.[2]

"This," Horner adds, "is in a sense the story of my life," but only "in a sense," since "the same life lends itself to any number of stories—parallel, concentric, mutually habitant, or what you will."[3] All stories, all interpretations, are arbitrary, and thus all are "in a sense" true.

Horner's viewpoint is contrasted with that of Joe Morgan, an instructor at the college. Morgan shares Horner's relativism but believes that action may be grounded in a personally, subjectively derived set of values. "In my ethics," he tells Horner, "the most a man can ever do is be right from his point of view." For Morgan the important thing is to be consistently faithful to the integrity of one's personal preferences, arbitrary though those preferences are: "There's no sense in apologizing, because nothing is ultimately defensible."[4] Morgan assumes the existence of an essential self, an irreducible core of needs and preferences to which appeal may be made as a basis for choice. But in a world without essences "nobody's authentic,"[5] as Horner points out. Like the atom, the self is infinitely divisible: "subjectivism doesn't really become intelligible until one finally locates the subject."[6] Indeed, the point has been made in the first sentence of the novel: "In a sense, I am Jacob Horner." The self is no less fragmented and problematical than anything else.

Horner's paralysis draws the attention of a mysterious physician, who undertakes to cure him. One of the remedies he prescribes is "mythotherapy," in which the patient is encouraged to invent myths, roles, and masks for himself and others.

2. *Ibid.*, p. 4.
3. *Ibid.*, p. 42.
4. *Ibid.*, p. 43.
5. *Ibid.*, p. 65.
6. *Ibid.*, p. 136.

As Horner puts it, "We are all casting directors a great deal of the time, if not always, and he is wise who realizes that his role-assigning is at best an arbitrary distortion of the actors' personalities."[7] Each person assigns flattering roles to himself and fictionalizes his relations with others in self-aggrandizing ways. The roles and fictions have no corresponding essence in the object, whether the object is one's own self or another's.

With the eclipse of an intelligible world of fixed essences, causal connections between events can no longer be assumed. Horner is incapable of explaining *why* he committed adultery. Or, rather, he is incapable of choosing among the infinite number of possible explanations which occur to him. Human experience is seen as fragmentary, disconnected, and ultimately incomprehensible. Reality is radically incommensurable with all ideas and judgments about it, leaving only the arbitrary and whimsical self-projections of mythotherapy as a basis of choice and action. The self is locked within a prison of its subjective myths from which there can be no possibility of escape.

The End of the Road in Poetic Theory

The End of the Road deals in a suggestive manner with an intellectual development of great consequence for modern philosophy and literature. In J. Hillis Miller's words, "modern thought has been increasingly dominated by the presupposition that each man is locked in the prison of his consciousness."[8] It would seem that many influential modern poetic critics and theorists find themselves in Jacob Horner's predicament with respect to the status of poetry. These writers tend to see human experience as inaccessible to rational understanding and

7. *Ibid.*, pp. 25–26.
8. *The Disappearance of God* (Cambridge: Harvard University Press, 1963), p. 8. Nietzsche defined the most characteristic quality of modern man as "the strange contrast between an inner life to which nothing outward corresponds, and an outward existence unrelated to what is within." (Quoted by Erich Heller, *The Artist's Journey into the Interior* [New York: Random House, 1965], p. 103.)

consequently are forced to fall back upon a conception of poetry as a kind of mythotherapy in order to avoid theoretical paralysis.

I. A. Richards' position, as set forth in *Science and Poetry*, provides an illustration of the problem. Richards writes:

> Ever since man first grew self-conscious and reflective he has supposed that his feelings, his attitudes, and his conduct spring from his knowledge. That as far as he could it would be wise for him to organise himself in this way, with knowledge as the foundation on which should rest feeling, attitude, and behaviour. In point of fact, he never has been so organised, knowledge having been until recently too scarce; but he has constantly been persuaded that he was built on this plan. . . . He has sought for knowledge, supposing that, . . . if he only knew what the world was like, this knowledge in itself would show him how to feel towards it, what attitudes to adopt, and with what aims to live.[9]

Richards does not say that all ideas and interpretations are arbitrary; on the contrary, he believes that real knowledge has been obtained. But this knowledge, "until recently too scarce," is strictly scientific in character; it consists of those empirical facts which are capable of quantification and laboratory verification. These facts are facts in disconnection dead and spiritless, telling us only how things behave and not what they truly are or how we ought to feel about them. Science has led to a "neutralisation of nature," according to which rational knowledge ceases to be a ground of value, for such knowledge entails no prescriptions for conduct, no basis for choice and action.

We appear to have been returned to Jacob Horner's predicament, but Richards is ready with a remedy:

> The remedy, since there is no prospect of our gaining adequate knowledge, and since indeed it is fairly clear that

9. *Science and Poetry*, (New York: W. W. Norton & Co., 1926), pp. 61–62.

genuine knowledge cannot serve us here and can only in-
crease our practical control of Nature, is to cut our pseudo-
statements free from belief, and yet retain them, in this
released state, as the main instruments by which we order
our attitudes to one another and to the world. . . . poetry
conclusively shows that even the most important among our
attitudes can be aroused and maintained without any belief
entering in at all.[10]

By pseudo-statements, of course, Richards means poetry, but
the term applies equally to expressions of value judgments,
prescriptions, and preferences. Richards' theory of the dual
functions of language follows from this dual conception of
experience: scientific statements describe the objective world
of neutral fact; emotive statements express the inner world of
values and preferences. The pseudo-statement, totally "free"
and independent of knowledge of objective states of affairs,
provides the necessary stimulus for emotional organization and
response and thereby rescues modern man from the loneliness
of a world in which nature has been neutralized and the
absolutes of traditional theology invalidated. Poetry, Richards
says in *Principles of Literary Criticism*, provokes in the reader
a "feeling of a revealed significance,"[11] even though nothing
objective need be revealed to him or even believed by him as
true. For our ability to be satisfied by such belief-feelings or
"objectless beliefs" is independent of our intellectual convic-
tions. "Opinion as to matters of fact, knowledge, belief, are
[*sic*] not necessarily involved in any of our attitudes to the
world in general or to particular phases of it." In fact, to base
attitudes on such opinion is "psychological perversion."[12] Thus
the only "truth" which poetry can legitimately claim is an
"emotive" or subjective truth. Without requiring actual belief,

10. *Ibid.*, p. 72.
11. *Principles of Literary Criticism*, (New York: Harcourt, Brace &
World, 1928), p. 283.
12. *Ibid.*, p. 281.

poetry allegedly can restore a sense of congeniality to a nature which, objectively viewed, we know to be indifferent to our aspirations.

Richards' views are echoed in the writings of innumerable modern critics. T. S. Eliot's admiration for the "mythical method" of *Ulysses* is grounded in his view that the objective correlatives of myth represent "a way of controlling, of ordering, of giving a shape and a significance to the immense panorama of futility and anarchy which is contemporary history."[13] That is to say, myth serves to impose an artificial coherence upon that which in reality has no coherence. Similarly, for Northrop Frye, the aim of poetry is not objective truth but rather the recovery of "that original lost sense of identity with our surroundings, where there is nothing outside the mind of man."[14] As with Richards, this "sense" of identity involves no actual belief. R. P. Blackmur applies these ideas in his essay, "The Later Poetry of W. B. Yeats." In a world which provides no objective, rational sanction for beliefs and values, Blackmur says, poets are forced to fall back upon the "emotional reality" of their privately constructed systems of "magic" and myth as a basis for poetic emotions: "the poet has to provide for himself in that quarter where authority and value are derived."[15] Eliot, of course, holds that the poet is better off when freed from the necessity to contrive his own personal myth, either because he lives in a period in which his myth is supplied by an existing social, philosophical, and religious order or because he has been able to recover the impersonal "tradition" still available even in the chaotic present. Nevertheless, Eliot and Blackmur are in agreement that the function of myth is to impose a satisfying but arbitrary scheme of order upon an

13. "Ulysses, Order, and Myth," in *The Modern Tradition*, ed. Richard Ellmann and Charles Feidelson, Jr. (New York: Oxford University Press, 1965), p. 681.

14. *The Educated Imagination* (Bloomington: Indiana University Press, 1964), p. 29.

15. *Language as Gesture* (New York: Harcourt, Brace & Co., 1952), p. 82.

incomprehensible world. Finally, Wallace Stevens, in much of his critical and poetic writing, represents the everyday world as a dead collection of disconnected particulars—"an extraneous object, full of other extraneous objects"[16]—in which the only order and unity are fabricated by the imagination. Stevens' description of modern poetry, "The poem of the mind in the act of finding/ What will suffice,"[17] suggests that poetry is the means by which the mind imposes upon reality whatever mythic scheme happens to "suffice" to satisfy the mind's craving for order. Poetry tells the mind, as the poem says, "that which it wants to hear." Since we can know nothing, or since nothing we can know makes any difference so far as the significance of choices and actions is concerned, it is left to the poet to create mythical structures which will at least answer to our desires. As Stevens writes elsewhere, echoing Richards, "In an age of disbelief, . . . it is for the poet to supply the satisfactions of belief, in his measure and in his style."[18]

The framework of assumptions in which human interpretations and values are seen as myths, subjectively willed creations which we impose upon an inert and inherently meaningless field of matter more or less to please ourselves, defeats the task of poetic theory. For once experience has become mythicized, the problem of the relationship between poetry and the external world can no longer be solved; indeed, the problem can scarcely be posed in meaningful form, since our very notion of an "external world" has been reduced to the status of merely another poetic fiction. Within such a framework, thought is an arbitrary exercise, judgment is beset by a hopeless relativism, and intellectual discussion and debate are little more than pointless shadowboxing. Speculation upon such subjects as poetic "truth"—the quotation marks become obligatory—becomes increasingly equivocal and evasive, for no area of specu-

16. *The Necessary Angel* (New York: Alfred A. Knopf, 1951), p. 151.
17. "Of Modern Poetry," *Collected Poems* (New York: Alfred A. Knopf, 1954), pp. 239–40.
18. *Opus Posthumous* (New York: Alfred A. Knopf, 1957), p. 206.

lation can be exempted from the shafts of a pervasive reflexive irony. But this mythic approach to experience persists in excluding from consideration the fact of the *coerciveness* of reality, that power possessed by objects outside of ourselves to compel human interpretations and judgments to move in one direction rather than another, that structure of determination in the object which tends to drive the relatively unprejudiced mind toward its conclusions. It is a matter of common experience that some viewpoints are manifestly more adequate, more mature, more genuinely called for by the reality of things than are other viewpoints.

Furthermore, the tendency to deny that intellectual beliefs can be a ground of values and responses produces a severe divorce between the emotional satisfactions of belief and the substance of belief. The notion, found in Richards, Stevens, and Frye, that poetry should supply the emotional benefits of belief without grounding them in an objective content to be believed *in* takes for granted the desirability of a psychic compartmentalization in the reader. He is required to engage in the *act* or *process* or *experience* of believing while discarding the *content* of the belief—as if he were to attempt to preserve the sensation or experience of nourishment while doing without the food. Even if it is conceded that the world is no more than "an extraneous object, full of other extraneous objects," it does not follow that our responses can be disengaged from our beliefs at will. Response, or at least response embodied in language, assumes a prior conceptual understanding of the nature of the context of experience to which the response is relevant; that is, responses are predicated upon beliefs about the features of the situation involved. Charles L. Stevenson, a philosopher who shares with Richards the emotivist premise that factual or descriptive arguments have no necessary connection with value judgments and attitudes, argues that "such a view does not cut off our evaluations from our scientifically established beliefs; for these beliefs, revealing the factual situation that presumably confronts us, normally make a vast difference to the sort of attitude that we express."[19] Even if we believe that the "factual situation" is meaningless, there is still *that* belief, and our attitudes will be predicated on it.

To follow the path of Richards and Frye by making poetic belief-feelings and their accompanying satisfactions independent of objective reality and truth is to convert poetry into a vehicle of sentimental wish fulfillment. One might justifiably reply to Richards that if the gratifications of his "objectless beliefs" are truly independent of "opinion as to matters of fact, knowledge, belief," then it is more dignified to do without such gratifications. If nature is really a dead field of neutral objects, then the best we can hope is to come to terms with that unfortunate fact as it is; there is no use urging the solace of mythotherapeutic constructions in which we do not even pretend to believe. The sentimental pleasure given by a mythic *sense* of identity between man and nature represents a desperate and futile evasion of the problem. If poetry serves only to tell the mind "that which it wants to hear," then poetry is trivial and we had best let the matter go at that.[20]

19. "On the Reasons that Can be Given for the Interpretation of a Poem," in *Philosophy Looks at the Arts,* ed. Joseph Margolis (New York: Charles Scribner's Sons, 1962), p. 129, n. 6. See also Stevenson's *Ethics and Language* (New Haven: Yale University Press, 1944), pp. 23, 88, 140–43. For an approach to the fact-value problem which attempts to go beyond the emotivism of Stevenson and show that "ethics can be based on evidence and that it is a matter of knowledge," see Henry B. Veatch, *Rational Man: A Modern Interpretation of Aristotelian Ethics* (Bloomington: Indiana University Press, 1962).

20. Erich Heller's comment defines the issue very well:

If it is not in the rationalistic pursuits of objective knowledge but only through the exercise of human affections that the question of values can be answered, can it then be answered at all? Is knowledge, gained in this way, not necessarily as elusive and as fickle, as deceptive and as unreliable, as are the human affections themselves? And if poetry is what we believe it to be, namely the affections' appeal to the affections, what sort of truth or value can there be in poetry? There is, it seems, an odd disparity between the seriousness with which poets view their profession, and the use to which it is put. . . . This has been the quixotic predicament of poetry . . . throughout the modern age. It came to a climax when rationalism and romanticism between them contrived to destroy the last remnants of a rational order of values (*The Disinherited Mind* [New York: Farrar, Straus and Cudahy, 1957], p. 270).

Poetry as Nonrational Knowledge

But it is undoubtedly reductive and unfair to equate the entire modern critical celebration of myth, symbol, and creative imagination with what Barth sardonically terms mythotherapy. For one thing, a substantial number of critics, Eliot himself among them, have taken issue with Richards' denial of the truth content of poetry and myth and have rejected Richards' openly therapeutic approach to poetics as cheapening.[21] The later New Critics and numerous mythopoeic critics have argued persistently that poetry is a mode of knowledge, a source of objective truth comparable to the truth of science. Such critics as Allen Tate, W. K. Wimsatt, and Philip Wheelwright have challenged Richards' restriction of knowledge to the practical and empirical realm and his positivist and emotivist conception of value. Far from seeing man as "locked in the prison of his own consciousness," without access to any knowledge relevant to his attitudes and values, forced back upon his self-imposed mythologies, these critics affirm the validity of a higher knowledge arrived at through imaginative activity and the contemplation of works of art.

And yet, on examination, the assumptions of those who have reacted vigorously against Richards' positivism turn out to be similar in many respects to those of Richards himself. The post-Ricardian New Critics, although they find Richards' view of *knowledge* much too confining, do not object to his narrowly restricted definition of *reason*. Instead of attacking Richards' positivism where it would seem to be most vulnerable, in its denatured, neutralized conception of reason and rational knowledge, these critics easily accede to this conception and thus are able to rehabilitate the concept of knowledge only by resorting to notions of poetic truth that are ill-defined, vague,

---

21. See *The Use of Poetry and the Use of Criticism* (London: Faber and Faber, 1933), pp. 121–42.

and mysterious. In rejecting the rational intelligibility of experience, the modern critic reduces the world to fragments and then is forced to seek a unifying principle in some form of mystical transcendence: Christian Incarnation (Eliot), mythic unconscious (Frye), vitalistic *élan* (Hulme), or linguistic paradox (Brooks).

Cleanth Brooks exemplifies the typically debased conception of reason when he writes of Keats's "Ode on a Grecian Urn" that the concluding proposition about beauty and truth is "not intended to be a generalization which can march out of the poem and take its place alongside the scientific and practical generalizations of the workaday world." Brooks adds that both Keats and Coleridge show a "reluctance to force didacticism. They respect the complexity of experience too much to violate it by oversimplification; the concrete, too much to indulge in easy abstractions. They think through their images."[22] Generalization is here identified with "scientific and practical" affairs of "the workaday world," as well as with oversimplification, didacticism, and "easy abstractions." These, by implication, line up in opposition to the "complexity of experience." Similarly, Brooks praises "The Canonization" for presenting "an idea or attitude which we have agreed, with our everyday logic, is false." Donne's "is not a logical proof," and it will not convince "the hard-boiled naturalist," yet it is a proof which the imagination embraces.[23] Brooks may appear to be repudiating not logic but "everyday logic," the presumably ossified and stereotyped thinking of "the hard-boiled naturalist." But there is no indication that Brooks recognizes the possibility of any other kind of logic. Logic itself is inherently "everyday," just as generalizations and abstractions are inherently "easy." Reason and rational discourse are synonymous with narrow-mindedness, formulaic reduction, banality, bourgeois conven-

22. *Modern Poetry and the Tradition* (Chapel Hill: University of North Carolina Press, 1939), p. 238.
23. *The Well Wrought Urn* (New York: Harcourt, Brace & Co., 1947), p. 193.

tionality, and a meanly practical spirit of calculation. As Erich Heller has observed with reference to certain passages in T. S. Eliot's criticism, abstract thought is assumed to be "the preoccupation of a group of men among whom the professional bores are in the majority."[24] One recalls Yeats's animadversions on "the shop-keeping logicians."

In this context, it is relevant to call attention to the extensive influence upon modern critical thought of T. E. Hulme and his popularization of the Bergsonian "Doctrine of Discontinuity," which enforces a severe ontological separation between the mechanical, the vital, and the moral or spiritual aspects of reality. The doctrine restricts the intellect to the province of mechanical and inorganic phenomena, refusing its competence to deal with the "intensive manifolds" in which experience is immediately given to consciousness.[25] From such a doctrine it is only a short step to Brooks's identification of logic with "the hard-boiled naturalist," or to Allen Tate's view that "experience has decided to ignore logic,"[26] or to John Crowe Ransom's strictures against Platonism, whose crime it is not only to distort and falsify "the rich, contingent materiality" of "the world's body" but actually to commit a kind of cold-blooded murder of it.[27]

Paradoxically, the Hulmean-Bergsonian doctrine of discontinuity is symptomatic of a deeper yearning for unity, that unity of seamless, continuous "intensive manifolds" which is overlooked by the rational mind but which can presumably be reconstituted within the organic wholeness of vision achieved by imagination or intuition. It is a clue to the strange equivocation of much current theorizing that the very critics who

24. *Disinherited Mind*, p. 150. See also Kathleen Nott's objections to the identification of reason with positivistic reductivism in *The Emperor's Clothes* (Bloomington: Indiana University Press, 1954), pp. 1–30.
25. *Speculations* (New York: Harcourt, Brace & Co., 1924), pp. 5–11, 173–214.
26. *The Man of Letters in the Modern World* (New York: Meridian Books, 1955), p. 335.
27. *The World's Body* (New York: Charles Scribner's Sons, 1938), pp. 122 ff.

reflect the influence of the doctrine of discontinuity by calling for a separation of poetry and ideas are the same who, in the next breath, preach the gospel of unity of sensibility, looking to poetry as a means of bringing "the whole soul of man into activity."[28] Rational formulations are presumed to be incompatible with organic unity of mind; but how can there be unity of mind if rational formulations are excluded? To exclude the discursive from poetry is to exclude a portion of the total human sensibility and to betray the ideal of unity.

Here is but one of the many anomalies which ensue for those critics who have adopted a self-defeating skepticism toward rational, discursive thought while yet persevering in their commitment to an ideal of knowledge and truth. If poetry does not assert ideas, how can it lay claim to an intellectual substance at all? The way that is usually sought out of this dilemma is to say that poetry "dramatizes" or "embodies" or "presents" or "realizes" ideas, but does not assert them. "Man can embody truth," says Yeats in a celebrated statement which reflects the assumptions underlying antipropositional poetics, "but he cannot know it."[29] Because one cannot know truth by rational means, one must not try to assert anything as objectively true but must "embody" within the self-sufficient context of one's poem the truth of a state of mind. But what does it mean to "embody truth"? Is it possible to "dramatize" an idea without asserting anything at all? It has not been shown how truth, whose very nature is tied up with predication and assertion, may be merely "presented" without any statemental import being involved.

---

28. Murray Krieger notes this inconsistency in the theories of Matthew Arnold, Eliot, and Richards: "They assert, on the one hand the need for a separation between ideas and poetry and, on the other hand, the need for a fusion and a unity in the poet's work" ("The Critical Legacy of Matthew Arnold," *Southern Review*, N.S., V [Spring, 1969], 473). See also Krieger's excellent discussion of the conflicts of New Critical theory in *The New Apologists for Poetry* (Minneapolis: University of Minnesota Press, 1956).

29. Quoted by Frank Kermode in *Romantic Image* (London: Routledge & Kegan Paul, 1957), p. 49.

In the ambiguity surrounding the concept of a kind of poetic meaning which is somehow "true" and yet not asserted or predicated of anything, we find an exemplification of the almost endless vacillation in which many contemporary critics have become involved as they attempt to affirm both the nonpropositional, nondiscursive character and the truth of poetry. Thus we find Brooks, on the one hand, condemning critics who go "outside the poem" by judging it against "abstract philosophical yardsticks" and, on the other hand, endorsing Eliot's statement that good poetry is "mature" and "founded on the facts of experience."[30] Obviously these latter criteria are not independent of determinations of empirical truth and falsity, and they cannot be applied without invoking "abstract philosophical yardsticks" derived from outside the poem, a procedure which implicitly acknowledges that the poem makes a kind of assertion. As Murray Krieger shows in *The New Apologists for Poetry,* the doctrines of contextual autonomy and "truth of coherence," which presuppose that the attribution of an assertive content to a poem violates the integrity of the imaginative experience, inevitably force the theorist into a flirtation with an elusive notion of poetic autotelism, an involvement from which he can extricate himself only by means of more or less violent self-contradiction. The assertions which were proscribed on one page in the interests of the poem's autonomy will have to be readmitted—covertly perhaps—on the next in the interests of the poem's claim to human relevance, "maturity," and "the facts of experience."

The root of the problem is that the desire of post-Ricardian New Critics to claim an objective knowledge for poetry conflicts with assumptions that preclude the very possibility of objective knowledge. If the formulations of reason have no relevance to the deeper realities of experience, and if poetry is not predicated on rational knowledge, then it is not clear on what grounds objective truth can be claimed. Consequently

30. *Well Wrought Urn*, p. 228.

there is an important sense in which poetry, even in the theories of such objectivist and absolutist critics as Eliot, Brooks, and Tate, becomes something not very different from the pseudo-statement—that is to say, mythotherapy—which it was in Richards. If poetic knowledge cannot be *asserted*, if it is not *about* anything, then one wonders how it can amount to more than the purely emotive or psychological "truth" which Richards concedes to effective pseudo-statements. Outside the mediating categories of rationality, logical relevance, and truth of correspondence, "experience" becomes nothing more than the chaotic flux of an infinite, undifferentiated subjectivity, and the theorist is obliged to concede a poetic "truth" to any mere dramatic exhibition of the flow of consciousness. The coalescent "truths" embodied in the presentation of "intensive manifolds" cannot be distinguished from subjective myths. In short, by repudiating the authority of reason and logic, the critic locks himself into Jacob Horner's solipsistic prison, his putatively objective poems affording at best a mythotherapeutic illusion of escape.

Coleridge and the Contemporary Dilemma

The tendency toward equivocation in contemporary definitions of poetic truth has its roots in the conflict between realist and idealist impulses which underlies romantic and modernist epistemology. This conflict is exemplified in the philosophical writings of Coleridge, from which so many modern critics have derived inspiration. Although Coleridge does not mean to denigrate rational understanding, he frequently vacillates over the question of the objectivity of knowledge. As he inquires, does the subjective "supervene to the objective" or vice versa?[31] Coleridge finally affirms "the absolute identity of subject and object,"[32] by which he means to reconcile the creative

31. *Complete Works*, ed. W. T. G. Shedd (New York: Harper & Brothers, 1853), III, 336.
32. *Ibid.*, p. 349.

and cognitive powers of the mind. Such an affirmation of identity, however, actually tips the balance in the direction of subjective idealism. If it is not permissible to make a realistic differentiation between subject and object, then there is no means by which we may avoid irrationalism. A world of coalescent perception, in which "we receive but what we give," in the language of "Dejection," is a world in which we have no way of distinguishing between what we are perceiving in the world outside of us and what we are creatively imposing upon that world. In such a state of affairs, the very concepts of knowledge and truth recede into indeterminacy.

One consequence of Coleridge's epistemological uncertainty is a corresponding confusion with respect to the issue of the autonomy of the creative imagination. According to Coleridge's concept of organic form, each poem is unique and incapable of being judged against any universal "abstract rule"; poems can be criticized only in terms of their "inappropriateness to their own end and being."[33] By erecting each poem into its own law, this doctrine tends to place the poem beyond criticism. As Paul Ramsey has noted in *The Lively and the Just*, Coleridge frequently appeals to the traditional, extrinsic "abstract rule" of logic, good sense, and rational coherence as the governing principles of poetry and criticism, thus violating his own organicist dictum that the imagination cannot be governed "from without."[34] This ambivalence foreshadows the New Critical vacillation between a realistic conception of objective truth and an idea of imaginative autonomy grounded in idealism.

But Coleridge's apparently self-contradictory attempt to affirm both realist and idealist viewpoints is rescued, after a fashion, by his commitment to a transcendentalist metaphysics

33. *Coleridge's Shakespearean Criticism*, ed. T. M. Raysor (London: Constable & Co., 1930), I, 224. The distinction between organic and "mechanic" form is borrowed from A. W. Schlegel.

34. *The Lively and the Just* (Tuscaloosa, Ala.: University of Alabama Press, 1962), pp. 24–25. The phrases from Coleridge appear in *Works*, III, 428–29.

grounded in a belief in a *Natur-geist* or Spirit of Nature. This Spirit of Nature, at once immanent and transcendent, infuses both subject and object and fuses them as one. The theory, as Coleridge says, "presupposes a bond between nature in the higher sense and the soul of man."[35] Under the protection of such a presupposition, the troublesome epistemological questions about the identity of subject and object lose their urgency, since subject and object, however undefined their boundaries, are seen to be in infallible correspondence anyway in that each participates in the same immanent-transcendent spiritual unity. The subjective myths engendered by the imagination correspond to a "nature in the higher sense," so that their claim upon reality is validated. The apparent contradiction between realism and idealism is reconciled within a higher unity. It is no longer necessary to be concerned about the problems of subjectivism, relativism, and anarchic irrationalism, since the Spirit of Nature, by embracing all experience and all consciousness, unifies any seemingly dissonant visions.

Coleridge's solution to these problems will not be convincing to the non-transcendentalist reader: it conjures away, rather than faces up to, the problem of subjectivism. But the theory makes coherent sense as long as we entertain the idea of a Spirit of Nature which holds the world together and unifies all potentially disparate subjectivities. It is somewhat baffling, on the other hand, to observe the struggles of contemporary organicists like Brooks, Hulme, and Murray Krieger, who attempt to maintain what is essentially a transcendentalist theory of creative imagination without clearly committing themselves to the transcendentalist metaphysics upon which the theory depends for its justification. Brooks, for instance, explaining why it is that poets "choose ambiguity and paradox rather than plain discursive simplicity," says: "It is not enough for the poet to analyse his experience as the scientist does,

35. *Works*, IV, 332.

breaking it up into parts, . . . His task is finally to unify experience. He must return to us the unity of the experience itself as man knows it in his own experience." But this unity, of course, is not a unity expressible or comprehensible in intellectual terms: "The poem, if it be a true poem is a simulacrum of reality . . . by *being* an experience rather than any mere statement about experience or any mere abstraction from experience."[36] Brooks is here attempting to speak in conceptual language about a unity which, by definition, transcends conceptual language.[37] Note the teasing ambiguity in the phrase, "unity of the experience." It is unclear whether the unity is one that inheres in objective reality or is merely a subjective *sense* of unity—like Richards' "feeling of a revealed significance." Or is there some intersubjective *Natur-geist* or transcendental ego presupposed here? Having denied the validity of abstract formulations and embraced Coleridge's transcendental faculty of imagination, Brooks does not venture an affirmation of the metaphysical doctrine which would be required to authenticate such a faculty. Unless we assume a bond between "nature in the higher sense and the soul of man," what can be the status of the unity to which Brooks refers? How can this unity be any more than a rhetorical solution to the problem of discontinuity between mind and nature? The solipsistic implications of Brooks's doctrines are not overcome.[38]

36. *Well Wrought Urn*, p. 194.
37. The New Critical logic which precipitates this dilemma is amusingly reconstructed by Morse Peckham:

> . . . poetry has a unique kind of semantic structure which reveals a unique kind of truth. Poetry says things which cannot be said in any other language. And what's more, we shall now tell you in non-poetic language what that meaning is which cannot be said in non-poetic language, though, for this reason, you must not imagine that you will know what that meaning is. That meaning can only be experienced; it cannot be known (*Man's Rage for Chaos; Biology, Behavior, and the Arts* [Philadelphia: Chilton Books, 1965], p. 127).

38. In Brooks and Wimsatt's *Literary Criticism: A Short History* (New York: Random House, 1957) Wimsatt declares that the "ironic and tensional theory" espoused by the authors is best grounded not within any of the "Platonic or Gnostic ideal world-views, or within the Manichaean full dualism and strife of principles," but rather within the

Contradiction as Truth

Murray Krieger's numerous works on poetic theory represent at once an illuminating analysis of the contradictions of New Critical organicism and the culminating embodiment of those very contradictions in a theory which enthrones contradiction and paradox as necessary and vital constituents of criticism.[39] Krieger writes of the dilemmas of post-Coleridgean poetics with candor, subtlety, and historical insight, yet he himself remains somewhat forlornly imprisoned in the logical traps which he analyzes so well. He asks: "Is not even the slight rational philosophic control of the stuff of drama infringement

---

"vision of suffering, the optimism, the mystery which are embraced in the religious dogma of the Incarnation" (p. 746). He does not elaborate, but it would appear that, for Wimsatt and Brooks, the mystery of the Incarnation has taken the place of the Coleridgean Spirit of Nature. To what extent this makes the validity of "the ironic and tensional theory" dependent upon the validity of Christian dogma is an open question.

It is interesting to consider the parallels between the issues troubling modern poetics and certain traditional theological problems. I have in mind here not only the reliance of contemporary critics upon quasi-mystical doctrines of unity; there is a further parallel between the critical appeal to "immediate experience," as the justification for poetry, and the Protestant doctrine of "justification by faith alone." In both instances, "external" criteria are deemed irrelevant—"correspondence" truth and moral adequacy in the case of poetics, "good works" in the case of theology. Jonathan Edwards, in his treatise *Religious Affections,* which deals with the problem of authenticating conversion experiences, encounters precisely the same problems as do critics who attempt to authenticate an "autonomous" poem. It is significant that Edwards is finally forced to fall back upon good works as "the principal evidence" of grace in order to avoid antinomianism (*Jonathan Edwards, Representative Selections,* rev. ed., ed. C. H. Faust and T. H. Johnson [New York: Hill and Wang, 1962], p. 252). Antinomianism, the doctrine which holds that the converted "saint" is an autonomous law unto himself and not bound by external law, is the theological counterpart of literary organicism. These parallels indicate that the critical tradition we have been examining may be closer to the spirit of Protestant individualism than would normally be supposed, given the strongly anti-Protestant, anti-individualistic temper of its leading exponents.

39. *New Apologists for Poetry; The Tragic Vision* (Chicago: University of Chicago Press, 1960); *A Window to Criticism* (Princeton, N. J.: Princeton University Press, 1964); *The Play and Place of Criticism* (Baltimore: Johns Hopkins Press, 1967).

enough to ensure the stacking of the cards, the intrusion of an abstract order that preexists the poem upon thematic oppositions?"[40] Because Krieger regards "rational, philosophic control" and "the stuff of drama" as antithetical, "abstract order" being at best an "intrusion" or gratuitous imposition upon reality, it follows that rational methods can represent for him only a "stacking of the cards," a timid and arbitrary shying away from what he terms the "Manichaean" complexity of the "raging existential world."[41] As W. K. Wimsatt has commented in a perceptive critique, the Manichaean complexity of things must be in some sense abstractly formulable, for otherwise Krieger would have been unable to say anything about it.[42] The problem here is that Krieger presupposes a metaphysics which guarantees the defeat of his theory, indeed of *any* theory, from the outset. Because he subscribes to the Bergsonian premise that experience is falsified by the rational and logical mind, Krieger's commitment to principles of coherence immediately refute themselves.[43] The raging existential world must spurn any such principles as a dishonest stacking of the cards—a cowardly concession to understanding in a world that has been defined beforehand as incomprehensible. Krieger stacks the cards against himself, in effect, and against theory in general, by adhering to premises which reduce any effort at understanding to bad faith and which force the theorist to

40. *Tragic Vision*, p. 240.
41. *Ibid.*, p. 247.
42. Included by Krieger in *Play and Place of Criticism*, pp. 195–218.
43. Krieger disclaims any ultimate philosophic assumptions. He warns that in speaking of the Manichaean nature of reality he is speaking "phenomenologically, not metaphysically." "What is being insisted upon here as Manichaean is not the ultimate nature of metaphysical or noumenal reality so much as the existential nature of that reality which makes itself dramatically available to the poet whose only commitment as poet is to experience and to the dramatic exigencies of his art" (*Tragic Vision*, p. 243). But why is the poet's "only commitment as poet" necessarily a commitment to the phenomenological disorder of experience and not to its "metaphysical" order? By simply assuming that the poet's chief responsibility is to dramatize "existential" fluidity, Krieger begs the question. See W. K. Wimsatt's criticisms in *Play and Place of Criticism*, pp. 217–18.

embrace contradictions as his only salvation. Poetic theory becomes an indulgence in the mysteries of paradox—the poem that is somehow both autotelic and referential, ordered and Manichaean.

This deliberate enthronement of contradiction underlies Krieger's recent appeal to "miraculism," a term which he borrows from Ransom and modifies. That is, it is simply a *miracle* that poetry is both referential and nonreferential, Manichaean and ordered—both a "window" through which can be viewed all the "desperate, unresolvable tensions" of reality and a "self-sufficient aesthetic system of intramural relations among symbols," which "inhibits an escape to the world." "The literary work . . . is able miraculously to satisfy both propositions at once, being at once totally thematic and totally aesthetic, answerable to itself only by being answerable to the outside world."[44] The theory of poetry has here become a kind of poetry, abandoning logical consistency as an unnecessary and unwelcome intrusion. It is in this spirit that Brooks speaks of "the paradox of the imagination itself," the fact that the imagination, inexplicably, is capable of reconciling that which to the eye of mere reason appears contradictory.[45] And Tate concludes a discussion of the problem of the coexistence of poetic autonomy and referentiality with the comment: "However we may see the completeness of poetry, it is a problem less to be solved than, in its full import, to be preserved."[46] In these

---

44. *Window to Criticism,* pp. 17–18. This sort of contradiction is paralleled in the arguments of certain existential philosophers. See J. M. Cameron's critique of Karl Jaspers' theory of "ciphers," "After the Fall," *New York Review of Books,* XI (August 1, 1968), 29.

45. *Well Wrought Urn,* pp. 17, 20.

46. *Man of Letters in the Modern World,* p. 63. A similar modesty with respect to the claims of criticism may be found in Hazard Adams' recent study, *The Interests of Criticism: An Introduction to Literary Theory* (New York: Harcourt, Brace & World, 1969):

. . . it appears that there is an ineradicable Romantic irony in the enterprise of criticism. Like the quest of the Byronic hero, it is endless and yet at the same time valuable—endless because its terms are finally self-defeating, and valuable because in its own inadequacy it calls attention to the greater adequacy of the poem itself, which manages to say or be more than remarks about it can ever say. For this reason

several instances, the theorist's contradictions are conceded to be incapable of logical resolution; yet it is implied that the contradictions are somehow valid, necessary, and profound, perhaps even more profound for being unresolvable—like the paradoxes of "The Canonization." In this way, the very desperateness of the theoretical contradictions becomes a badge of the critic's integrity—proof of the extent to which he refuses to compromise his vision of the complexities and conflicts, "the desperate, unresolvable tensions" of experience. The theorist's aim becomes not to "solve" theoretical problems so much as to "preserve" them in all their rich, tensional duality—to preserve them above all from the inherent dishonesty and falsification of logical solution. Thus the critic's theory, like the autonomous poem which it sanctifies, becomes a law unto itself, invulnerable to the cavils of the shopkeeping logicians.

Reason, Assertion, and Poetry

To sum up: antipropositionalist poetics, by defining poetry as dramatic presentation upon which rational statements are not allowed to intrude, tends to reduce poetry to a form of mytho-therapy. The typical opposition between propositional and presentational meaning renders the theorist's well-intentioned appeals to the world of objective reality illegitimate and induces him to obscure the distinction between what is true and what is desirable. The separation of poetry and ideas tends to destroy the unity of humanistic knowledge, intensifying the fragmentation which the theory originally set out to repair. It

---

it is possible to characterize criticism as fundamentally negative. It is always denying the adequacy of any critical statement and constantly urging us to look again . . . (p. 141).

The reference to what the poem "manages to say" here is anomalous since Adams insists throughout his book that a poem "can only mean itself," that "it *means* only what it *is*, and therefore it has *being* rather than *meaning*" (p. 111). Since criticism is the realm of "meaning," not "being," it follows that criticism can say nothing at all about the poem, although Adams does not acknowledge this implication of his argument.

should be clear that the chief assumptions underlying this kind of theory need to be reexamined.

The view that poetry "presents" a kind of immediate, non-discursive meaning seems to me to do considerable violence to the nature of language. For language, I would argue, cannot achieve significance of any kind without the mediation of abstract concepts that are separable from the experiences and objects they intend. Although it cannot be denied that poetic meaning contains extrapropositional or extraconceptual elements, language can never be wholly deprived of conceptual meaning without surrendering coherence. Organic theorists fail to recognize how limited the capacity of language is to depart from its linear, consecutive, categorical, and mediating characteristics, how feeble an instrument language is—in comparison with other media like painting, sculpture, and dance—if one is primarily interested in the reproduction of experience without the intervention of abstract frameworks of thought. Even the most "organic" forms of language constantly and irrepressibly convey implications of abstract meanings. The expectation that language deal with experience without conceptual mediation leads to a disillusioned skepticism toward language and eventually to a repudiation of verbal art itself.

But even if it is conceded that poetic meanings are in some measure conceptual and propositional meanings, some will continue to deny that poetic meanings constitute *assertions* about matters outside the poem. The poem, they argue, although it may employ conceptual modes of discourse, is an autonomous, self-sufficient organism which wholly contains its own meaning within itself. I would reply that the act of using language within the heightened, intensified medium of verse carries with it an unavoidable assumption of referential liability. The poet, regardless of what type of poet he is, implicitly reveals some view of experience. He cannot help saying something about the human situation in general, cannot avoid incurring the risks of assertion. It is arbitrary to limit the liability of his statement by claiming that his poem's meaning is "about the poem itself."[47] Such a claim can scarcely do justice to the high value which men have always placed upon poetry, and it can give no explanation of the presence of important human subject matter in the greatest poetry. How could we explain the fact that, as Melville points out, "No great and enduring volume can ever be written on the flea"?[48] To be sure, much poetry conveys its statements indirectly, by implications rather than overt propositions. But implied statements are statements nevertheless and invite application to reality.

However, most contemporary critics will grant that poetic meanings bear some ultimate relationship to the world of human experience. It is my contention that this relationship

47. There is, to be sure, a legitimate sense in which a work of literature may be said to be "about itself," but this sense does not imply that such a work makes no statement. All works of any complexity are cross-referential within themselves: e.g., the speeches of the chorus in a Greek tragedy refer to events and characters within the plot of the play. In certain modern works, where the element of cross-reference becomes particularly intricate, elaborate, and self-conscious, there occurs what Joseph Frank calls "the principle of reflexive reference" (*The Widening Gyre* [New Brunswick, N.J.: Rutgers University Press, 1963], pp. 12–14). As it is employed by such writers as Proust, Pound, Joyce, Eliot, and Djuna Barnes, the principle of reflexive reference is seen by Frank as functioning to shut off external reference by means of a spatialization of form which upsets the older conventions of linear, discursive, temporal narrative or expository sequence. Frank's account of "spatial form" is illuminating, but the question is whether reflexive reference can wholly circumvent or displace external reference, and Frank, at least in an earlier version of his account, acknowledges that it cannot. In the original version of the essay, "Spatial Form in Modern Literature," Frank says that his explanation of the principle of reflexive reference is an "extreme statement of an ideal condition rather than of an actually existing state of affairs" (*Sewanee Review*, LIII [Spring, 1945], 230). The qualification is omitted from the later version of the essay incorporated in *The Widening Gyre*. For a critique of the concept of spatial form and the antihistorical tendencies of "mythicism," see Philip Rahv, *The Myth and the Powerhouse* (New York: Noonday Press, 1966), pp. 14–21.

Works which are said to be "about themselves" frequently may be discovered to imply statements about the conditions of human perception, the difficulties of distinguishing appearance from reality, and other epistemological statements.

48. *Moby-Dick* (New York: Bobbs-Merrill, 1964), p. 580.

entails statements, that it cannot be satisfactorily explained solely in terms of the concepts of the "enactment" or "embodiment" of experience. In fact, the antithesis of statement and enactment is finally unreal. There is no good reason why the statement or implication of propositional assertions and the dramatization of processes of mind should be viewed as mutually exclusive purposes of language. Like other verbal forms, poems tend *both* to assert propositions and dramatize states of mind at the same time. But this is not to argue that poetry should be conceived as statement plus an attached increment of separable decoration or ornament, the view which antipropositional theorists often attribute to their opponents. The conceptual statements made by a poem are functionally connected to the enacted attitudes in a ground-consequent relationship. If the attitudes are intelligible, they are grounded in conceptual objects, which means that the dramatically enacted and the conceptually asserted aspects of the poem are unified. No theorist committed to the ideal of the organic unity of poetry can afford to sever statement from dramatic presentation and to cast the two as adversaries.

The poem which I have chosen in order to illustrate these generalizations is Wallace Stevens' "The Course of a Particular":

Today the leaves cry, hanging on branches swept by wind,
Yet the nothingness of winter becomes a little less.
It is still full of icy shades and shapen snow.

The leaves cry . . . One holds off and merely hears the cry.
It is a busy cry, concerning someone else.
And though one says that one is part of everything,

There is a conflict, there is a resistance involved;
And being part is an exertion that declines:
One feels the life of that which gives life as it is.

The leaves cry. It is not a cry of divine attention,
Nor the smoke-drift of puffed-out heroes, nor human cry.
It is the cry of leaves that do not transcend themselves,

> In the absence of fantasia, without meaning more
> Than they are in the final finding of the ear, in the thing
> Itself, until, at last, the cry concerns no one at all.[49]

Contemporary theory, in the main, would hold that such generalized propositions as "There is a conflict, there is a resistance involved;/And being part is an exertion that declines," although they might constitute philosophical generalizations if abstracted from the poem, ought not to be read as such within the poetic context itself. For in the first place, the propositions function as a partial aspect of the dramatic persona's total response to his situation. The philosophical ideas are given as aspects of a particular experience, not advanced as the conclusions of a theoretical treatise. Rather than assert a world-view, they exemplify "what it feels like" to hold a world-view—in a particular situation. Secondly, any declarative thrust which the propositions may possess is ultimately cancelled by the qualifying pressure of the total surrounding context. And finally, it is simply never the *purpose* of a poem to assert a proposition. To read the propositions of any poem as if they were assertions about external reality is to violate the integrity of the poem by confusing its methods and aims with those of practical modes of communication and to invite the application of inappropriate criteria of judgment. The truth or falsity of the poem's generalizations, as generalizations, is irrelevant to the validity of the poem. If any truth is actually claimed by the poem, it is not a propositional truth of correspondence, but a truth enacted and experienced, referential in a reflexive manner to the self-contained world of the poem itself.

49. *Opus Posthumous,* pp. 96–97. "Ear," in the penultimate line is misprinted as "air" in *Opus Posthumous* and most subsequent printings. For the original (and correct) text, see *Hudson Review,* IV (Spring, 1951), 22. The error was first noted by Yvor Winters in a 1959 Postscript to *In Defense of Reason* (Denver: Alan Swallow, 1947), p. 459. For further discussion, see Richard A. Macksey, "The Climates of Wallace Stevens," in *The Act of the Mind: Essays on the Poetry of Wallace Stevens,* ed. Roy Harvey Pearce and J. Hillis Miller (Baltimore: Johns Hopkins Press, 1965), p. 216, n. 17.

Let us grant that there is something to be said for this way of looking at the poem. Certainly, such an approach provides a corrective to the common tendency to read poetry for its message alone and to ignore the obliquities and complications wrought by the linguistic context. The propositions in question in Stevens' poem *are* embedded in an action dramatically rendered, a fact which conditions the way in which they must be read. Nevertheless, to recognize the importance of the dramatic context is not necessarily to limit the liability of the poem's propositions or to reduce the extent to which they assert something about the human situation, something which invites application to contexts of experience outside the poem. There is no reason to discard the natural and obvious view that the poem does assert its propositions in a manner which makes an unmistakable claim upon objective truth of correspondence and that the validity of this truth claim ought to be a relevant consideration in the critic's judgment of the poem as a poem. Whether the propositions are actually true or false in this instance may be debated, but that is not the point. The point is that the poem *asks* that these propositions be received as true statements.

"The Course of a Particular" asserts that the human situation is one of isolation amid an alien nature, a nature symbolized by the dead leaves which "do not transcend themselves" by communicating a meaning and whose cry "concerns no one at all." Nature is a mere congeries of particulars, which simply *are*, which convey no Arcadian or pantheistic message of solace to the beholder. Or, rather, that is how the protagonist sees nature "in the absence of fantasia," of the imagination which might, if it were operative in him, impose a satisfying subjective order and meaning upon the particulars. But the speaker, although he longs to be "part of everything," finds that his ability to project his personality onto nature gradually declines as his imagination comes into conflict with the impersonal emptiness of the objective world. By asserting all this, the poem attempts to define the conditions of human life, to convey an understanding of what the score is. In asserting these propositions, the poem shares an important characteristic with nonpoetic, expository types of utterance.

At the same time, although it does assert generalizations, the poem differentiates itself from nonpoetic discourse by making systematic use of the rhythmical potentialities of language. It exploits these rhythmical potentialities in order to dramatize a state of mind, an attitude, with respect to the situation it defines. For instance, one of the poem's notable technical features is the employment of a long, undulating, six- and seven-stress line, freighted with long vowels and frequent clusters of sounded consonants, all of which tend to retard the rhythmic movement and suggest, in conjunction with the conceptual elements of the poem, a sense of heaviness and emotional attrition as well as deep longing. By means of this significant pattern of movement, Stevens' protagonist is made to *act out* the gradual decline of his "exertion" to be "part of everything." But why should this kind of dramatic enactment of experience be viewed as in any way antithetical to assertion? The poem "presents" its enacted attitudes only with reference to what it asserts about the world. The dramatized attitudes reflected in the style and movement are *intentional:* they are "about" the context of experience whose features are objectively predicated through the asserted content of the poem. The extrapropositional elements, in other words, are logically grounded in abstract conceptualization which refers to external experience. Like other forms of discourse, poems tend, either overtly or by implication, to advance predications about the human situation, and their internal coherence of attitude is dependent upon the coherence of the predications. No less than a human being, a poem achieves no coherent, stable identity as an entity "in itself" unless it establishes a relationship to the world outside itself.

But what about the problem presented by the qualifying forces exerted upon the generalizations by the total linguistic context? For example, is not the proposition "being part is an

exertion that declines" so qualified by the pressure of its surrounding tensions that it ceases to operate as an assertion?
Consider the implication of Stevens' attributing a "cry" to the
leaves; does not this personification of nature conflict with the
assertion that nature is impersonal? Although the disparity is
significant, it does not follow that the argument of the poem is
cancelled or subverted. Through the device of personification,
the poem implies that the speaker *longs for* the solace of a
humanized, personified nature, even as he recognizes that any
such solace is illusory. In the act of asserting an idea with
tragic implications, the poem betrays a wish to believe the
contrary, to evade these implications. Admittedly, then, the
propositional thrust of the poem is powerfully *influenced* by
its dramatic context. However, the influence in this case works
in the direction of reinforcing, enriching, and deepening the
content of the propositions, and not of negating or contraven-
ing them.[50] The attitude of longing and despair, suggested by
the rhythmic movement and intensified by the wishful personification, supplies a concrete emotional and psychological ma-
trix from which the abstract propositions draw a heightened
significance. We have not merely a definition of man's position
of separation from things, but the dramatized sense of what
that separation entails emotionally. The abstract assertion
about the emptiness of nature is invested with a sense of "what
it feels like" to be lost amid such emptiness. The complex
blend of resignation and longing communicated by the total
context enriches and completes the conceptual propositions,
but their asserted content remains intact. An adequate theory
would have to recognize this element of assertion in the
poem.

One reason why the presence of conceptual assertion in
poetry is so seldom acknowledged lies in the fact that much of
the poetry written since the romantic period has taken as its

50. Even when an ironic "undercutting" of positions takes place in a
poem, this does not mean that the poem contains no ultimate assertion.
See below, pp. 92, 113–18.

theme the inadequacy of rational thought. It is all too easy to take such antirationalistic poetry on its own terms and thus to ignore the large extent to which it continues to depend upon those old-fashioned modes of communication which it aims to discredit. When we say that a particular poem depicts an "irrational world" or a "suprarational unity," we should not suppose that we have said anything to deny that the poem makes a conceptual statement. The poem which suggests that human experience is chaotic and full of contradictions, that, as Dostoevski's underground man puts it, "man everywhere and always, whoever he may be, has preferred to act as he wished and not in the least as his reason and advantage dictated," must be held liable for an assertion about reality, regardless of how indirect its presentation. Even the view that "each man is locked in the prison of his own consciousness" purports to give an objective description of the human situation in rational terms. The discrediting of teleological conceptions of history, of the concept of an ordered, harmonious, purposive cosmos, does not necessarily imply the bankruptcy of rational discourse. But when the subject matter of a poem is the absence of a rational end in the universe, it is tempting to conclude that the poem must be ordered by some nonrational principle.

This confusion accounts for the frequently striking inconsistency between the theories of antipropositionalists and their interpretations of specific poems. Thus, J. Hillis Miller on Stevens:

> The death of the gods exists not only as Stevens' theoretical presupposition, but in the intimate texture of his verse. His images entirely contain their own reality. They are not symbolic. They are what they are. In this they are like physical objects, for these too, in Stevens' world, do not have meaning, nor do they point toward some ideal world which they signify. Natural objects and poetic images simply exist. "A poem need not have a meaning and like most things in nature often does not have."

But if we turn back a page, we find Miller writing in a wholly different vein about Stevens' poetry:

> Leaves, flames, peacocks, planets; glade-boat, water, rainbows, birds. . . . Each image in "Domination of Black" or "The Load of Sugar-Cane" is another case of the universal turning or flowing. There is no progression from one to another, and each has the same quality of firstness. It is as if the reader were facing the spatial representation of a temporal sequence of metamorphosis, or, one might say, it is like the universe of Heraclitus.[51]

In this passage, despite what Miller said in the remarks previously quoted, it is evident that Stevens' images *do* convey a meaning. This meaning is that things have no meaning. Leaves, flames, peacocks, etc., are subsumed under a generalized concept of which they constitute—in Miller's own words—a "case": the Heraclitean theory of "the universal turning or flowing." The images are not merely "what they are" but are illustrative of an idea, just as surely as are the images of Pope or Dryden. The critic is apparently prevented from noticing the inconsistency because the tenor of the poem obscures it.

Thus it may be more true to say that the recognition of the assertive and abstractly philosophical characteristics of poetry has not really disappeared from criticism but has been obscured by a tendentious critical vocabulary. In a period in which previously orthodox and conventional opinions are being rapidly overthrown, critical theories often only *seem* to make a separation between poetry and abstract doctrines. On investigation, it can be seen that what is really being denied is the connection between poetry and those doctrines which are *conventionally* held to be true, that is to say, those which the critic believes to be false: e.g., scientific naturalism, realistic epistemology, rationalistic ethics, etc. Or, rather, it is only the

51. *Poets of Reality* (Cambridge: Harvard University Press, 1965), pp. 227–28.

discarded conventional platitudes which are given the labels "belief" and "doctrine." The beliefs and doctrines held by the critic and applauded when discovered in poetry (e.g., the paradoxical nature of experience, the "unity of being," etc.) are designated by the more honorific title of "vision" and held to be beyond the scope of rational understanding, which is arbitrarily identified with conventional beliefs.

Hesitant about the status of such metaphysical concepts as "truth," "reality," and "objectivity," contemporary critics have unfortunately tended to take refuge from the legitimate problems posed by these terms in an evasive and self-protective rhetoric. To speak of images which "entirely contain their own reality" is to create the suggestion that abstract categories have in some way been transcended or bypassed and to give reassurance that the poem can be removed from those doctrinal contexts which are felt to be puzzling or distasteful. Such rhetoric insinuates to the unwary reader that questions like "What does this poem say?" and "Can I believe this to be true?" are the sort asked only by Philistines. But such questions have always been prominent in the great critics, and we need a critical vocabulary which permits them to be asked openly once more. Only under such a condition can we arrive at a theory which makes of poetry something more than a form of mythotherapy.[52]

52. Although many of these theories have become identified with specific schools of academic criticism, particularly the New Criticism, it is noteworthy that the antithesis of statement and dramatic presentation appears repeatedly in pronouncements of leading spokesmen of avant-garde aesthetics from Ezra Pound and Antonin Artaud to Charles Olson, Alain Robbe-Grillet, and Susan Sontag. Pound's theory of the ideogram and of "ideas in action" and Artaud's concept of "metaphysics in action" foreshadow the antirationalistic invocations of organic thinking and "thinking through images" which have come to typify the writings of conservative academic theorists. Miss Sontag's strictures "against interpretation" ("to interpret is to impoverish, to deplete the world . . .") and against ideological conceptions of art, although often aimed against academic fashions, are logical extensions of that skepticism and hostility toward analytic thought which have long marked the major schools of

---

academic criticism. She holds that "a work of art encountered as a work of art is an experience, not a statement or an answer to a question. Art is not only about something; it is something. . . . the knowledge we gain through art is an experience of the form or style of knowing something rather than a knowledge of something (like a fact or a moral judgment) in itself" (*Against Interpretation* [New York: Farrar, Straus & Giroux, Inc., 1967], pp. 7, 21). Such statements might easily have appeared thirty years ago in the pages of the *Sewanee Review.*

CHAPTER TWO

I. A. Richards:
Emotive Autonomy

In the previous chapter we discussed I. A. Richards' theory of poetry as pseudo-statement and his view that objective truth and cognitive belief are irrelevant to poetic appreciation. The present chapter will explore these matters in somewhat greater detail, examining further implications of Richards' distinction between scientific and emotive language. Finally, we raise the question of whether Richards changed his views, as has been argued by some, with respect to the relationship between poetry and truth.

The Two "Uses" of Language

Although Richards considers poetry to be an "emotive" use of language, we should not suppose him to mean that it is devoid of intellectual reference and meaning, as some commentators have thought. Most instances of emotive language, Richards says, contain references, and he is severe with readers who fail to construe the "sense" of a poem accurately. Pseudo-statements are "pseudo" not because they are incoherent or fail to make sense intellectually but because the referential truth or falsity of the sense they contain has no bearing upon their value and effectiveness. "The questioning, verificatory way of handling [the references in a poem] is irrelevant, and in a competent reader it is not allowed to interfere."[1] When Richards says that the greatest poets "refrain from assertion," he is denying not the presence of propositional elements in poetry but rather their applicability to the objective world. To make true statements about the world is not the "function" or "use" of an emotive statement.

According to the emotive theory of meaning popularized by such positivists as Schlick, Carnap, and Ayer, most of the statements of ethics, theology, and metaphysics are not literally significant, since they fail to meet the so-called verifiability criterion of meaning.[2] Ayer, for example, argues that "metaphysical statements" are not meaningful as assertions, although they are likely to be emotionally significant to the speaker and may give information about his tastes and preferences.[3] Richards sometimes speaks of poetry in these terms, as if it were a kind of literal nonsense. But he concedes that empirically verifiable, and hence literally significant, propositions do frequently appear in poems. His overriding point, however, is that since the verifiability of the references in such cases is irrelevant to the value of the emotive attitudes which they serve to stimulate, the question of whether or not the references constitute an empirical or metaphysical proposition simply need never arise. Poems, of course, *can* be, and unfortunately often *are*, read as if they conveyed assertions about

1. *Principles of Literary Criticism* (New York: Harcourt, Brace & World, 1928), p. 268.
2. Some representative statements are: Rudolf Carnap, "The Elimination of Metaphysics through the Logical Analysis of Language"; Morritz Schlick, "The Turning Point in Philosophy"; "What is the Aim of Ethics?"; and A. J. Ayer, "Verification and Experience," all collected in *Logical Positivism*, ed. A. J. Ayer (New York: Free Press, 1959). See also Ayer, *Language, Truth and Logic* (New York: Dover Publications, 1952).
3. *Language, Truth and Logic*, p. 35.

morality, society, and life in general, but to read them in this way is to fail to treat poetry as poetry—to *use* it improperly. In this respect, Richards' view is close to Northrop Frye's argument that "the artist uses ideas, but *qua* artist is not otherwise concerned with their truth,"[4] as well as Susanne K. Langer's view that, although the "material of poetry is discursive, . . . the product—the artistic phenomenon—is not."[5] "If direct statements occur in a good poem," says Mrs. Langer, "their directness is a means of creating a virtual experience, a non-discursive form expressing a special sort of emotion or sensibility; that is to say, their *use* is poetic even if they are bald assertions of fact."[6]

The idea that a verbal utterance is capable of being "used" in numerous ways and that the kind of meaning ascribed to it depends upon the particular purpose to which it is put has been developed most notably in modern philosophy by Wittgenstein and popularized by the Logical Positivists of the Vienna Circle and a later, less homogeneous group of analytic philosophers. The thinkers associated with the Vienna group, influenced by the early Wittgenstein of the *Tractatus*, emphasize the opposition between verifiable, meaningful statements and metaphysical pseudo-statements. The analysts, influenced by the later Wittgenstein of the *Philosophical Investigations*, tend to be critical of the oversimplifications of the positivists and to see more varied uses in language than are allowed for by the empirical-metaphysical dichotomy. The "ordinary language" approach in particular stresses the complex variety of the uses of everyday forms of language and warns against inflexible categorizations and misleading dichotomies.

The ordinary language philosopher J. L. Austin proposes a distinction between the "constative" or statemental use of an

4. *Fearful Symmetry* (Boston: Beacon Press, 1962), pp. 27–28.
5. *Philosophy in a New Key*, 2d ed. (New York: New American Library, 1961), p. 221.
6. *Feeling and Form* (New York: Charles Scribner's Sons, 1953), p. 228.

utterance, its use in reporting facts held as true, and the "performative" use, where the utterance itself is a part of the "doing of an action," as in a ceremony, a promise, or an oath. "When I say, before the registrar or altar, etc., 'I do,' I am not reporting on a marriage: I am indulging in it."[7] Austin lists several kinds of performative uses, among which are "verdictives" (estimating, reckoning, appraising, giving verdicts, etc.); "exercitives" (appointing, voting, ordering, urging, advising, warning, etc.); and "commissives" (promising, vowing, wagering, announcing an intention, etc.).[8] All of these represent uses of language distinct from the purely constative. This distinction between constatives and performatives invites comparison with contemporary literary critical distinctions between propositional discourse and the dramatic actions of poetry. However, Austin refrains from making constative and performative uses independent of each other. He repeatedly warns that in many instances the distinction between constative and performative uses is difficult to draw, that these uses overlap considerably, and that unadulterated forms of the above categories are seldom found. (Indeed, as Austin comments, the term "use" itself, in this context, "is a hopelessly ambiguous or wide word."[9]) Although a sentence beginning "I promise" or "I apologize" will be used as a performative and is therefore not properly true or false, such a sentence nevertheless *implies* or *presupposes* a number of constatives: such performatives imply that "it is true and not false that I am committed to doing something subsequently."[10] The true-false considerations which apply to the assessment of constatives are not irrelevant to the assessment of performatives. Unlike Richards and Mrs. Langer, Austin does not attempt to sever the consideration of

7. *How to Do Things with Words*, ed. J. O. Urmson (New York: Oxford University Press, 1965), p. 6.
8. *Ibid.*, pp. 150 ff.
9. *Ibid.*, p. 100.
10. *Ibid.*, pp. 45–46. See also John R. Searle, "How to Derive 'Ought' from 'Is,'" in *Theories of Ethics*, ed. Philippa Foot (New York: Oxford University Press, 1967), p. 101–14.

the truth content of utterances from that of their performance or effect.

Erich Heller, in *The Disinherited Mind*, offers a number of good criticisms of the doctrine of the poetic "uses" of ideas as it is expounded in the criticism of T. S. Eliot. Eliot says, in a famous comment, that "neither Shakespeare nor Dante did any real thinking—that was not their job"; rather they used for aesthetic ends the currents of thought predominant in their age. "Dante, *qua* poet, did not believe or disbelieve the Thomist cosmology or theory of the soul: he merely made use of it, or a fusion took place between his initial emotional impulses and a theory, for the purpose of making poetry."[11] Heller raises the question of whether it is possible "to 'use' thought without thinking in the process of using it." "For thought," he points out, "is not an object but an activity, and it is impossible to 'use' an activity without becoming active. One can use a table without contributing to its manufacture; but one cannot use thinking or feeling without thinking and feeling."[12] We may infer from Heller's criticisms that it is arbitrary to single out a particular use of a statement as the peculiarly aesthetic or poetic use and to hold that other ends the statement appears to fulfill must be negligible or incidental. Such conclusions appear to be derived more from theories about the needs of modern culture—particularly the need for some emotional equivalent of religious faith and ritual—than from a consideration of the nature of poetry itself. Mrs. Langer's assumption, which has its counterpart in Richards' theory, that the intelligence of modern man is "keen but precarious" and hence in need of a strong dose of "metaphysical myth, régime, and ritual expression"[13] serves as the foundation of an a priori approach to the concept of the poetic "use" of language, as axioms concerning the ultimate uses of poetry in a supposedly overintellectualized

11. *Selected Essays* (New York: Harcourt, Brace & Co., 1950), pp. 116–18.

12. *The Disinherited Mind* (New York: Farrar, Straus and Cudahy, 1957), p. 151.

13. *Philosophy in a New Key*, p. 242.

culture are permitted to take precedence over aspects of poems evident to observation and common sense.

"Experience Is its Own Justification"

Richards' doctrine of the two uses of language must be examined in the context of his "psychological theory of value," according to which value is equated with emotive satisfaction and deprived of any connection with objective knowledge. In this theory, the "grounds" of an emotion become, in effect, the emotion itself; emotion and value must become "self-supporting" and "sufficient to themselves" in order to survive.[14] "The justification of any attitude *per se* is its success for the needs of the being. It is not justified by the soundness of the views which may seem to be, and in pathological cases are, its ground and causes."[15] Only a "pathological case" would try to adduce *good reasons* for an attitude, to ground it in sound opinion. "In brief," Richards asserts, "experience is its own justification."[16]

The key to this position may be found in Richards' theory of the nervous system as an ever-shifting organization of a multitude of "interests" and "needs" which is constantly seeking to move from a state of disequilibrium to one of equilibrium. The responses which the system makes to each state of disequilibrium are the "impulses," and the satisfaction of these impulses restores equilibrium to the system. "Attitudes" are the "outward going part" of the impulsive response, "the impulses toward one kind of behaviour or another which are set ready by the response."[17] Those particular states of equilibrium are most valuable which involve the participation of the greatest number of needs, impulses, and attitudes—those most inclusive of "fullness of life." "That organisation [of impulses] which is least wasteful of human possibilities is, in

14. *Science and Poetry* (New York: W. W. Norton & Co., 1926), p. 76.
15. *Principles of Literary Criticism*, p. 281.
16. *Science and Poetry*, p. 79.
17. *Ibid.*, p. 28.

short, the best."[18] The most fulfilling behavior, and hence the most effective poem, engages "a maximum of varied satisfactions," while demanding "a minimum of suppression and sacrifice," so that the best poetry is likely to be invulnerable to irony.[19] The doctrine echoes Coleridge's view that the poet "brings the whole soul of man into activity," and it anticipates the emphasis upon ironic inclusion and complexity in later theories. This ethics of inclusion provides Richards with a further justification for denying the poem's capacity to make an assertion: assertion "involves suppressions, of indefinite extent, which may be fatal to the wholeness, the *integrity* of the experience."[20] The idea that assertion is repressive of psychic energies corresponds to the doctrine, discussed in Chapter One, that rational formulations falsify reality.

Richards claims that his doctrine of fullness and balance has established a normative standard for evaluating poems and other emotive experiences, a standard which is independent of absolutist ethical assumptions. It is evident, however, as Eliseo Vivas points out, that such qualities as fullness, waste, and suppression are themselves absolute goods and evils in Richards' system.[21] Furthermore, as critics of Richards have suggested and as Richards himself sometimes admits, his criteria are incapable of being applied with any confidence to concrete ethical situations. For example, Richards says that "unfair or aggressive behaviour, and preoccupation with self-regarding interests . . . lead to a form of organisation which deprives the person so organised of whole ranges of important values. . . . Swindling and bullying . . . have their cost. . . . And the greater part of the cost lies . . . in actual systematic disability to attain important values."[22] Richards does not say how the presumably more "important" and valuable types of organiza-

18. *Principles of Literary Criticism*, p. 52.
19. *Ibid.*, pp. 53, 250.
20. *Ibid.*, p. 276.
21. *Creation and Discovery* (Chicago: Henry Regnery Co., 1955), pp. 337–38.
22. *Ibid.*, pp. 53–54.

tion can be shown to be more "full of life" than the swindler's satisfactions in taking advantage of his victims. Nor does he provide any clue as to how the "unity" of an experience can be authenticated. He admits that the experimental techniques which would presumably allow him to measure the degree of unity and fullness of an experience are not yet available. Hence, although it may be conceded that whole ranges of values are overlooked by the swindler and the bully, there is no way of assuring ourselves that the sensitive, honest, and unself-ish organization is not itself being deprived of whole ranges of values, namely, the considerable satisfactions it might be deriv-ing from aggression, swindling, and bullying. Richards' psy-chological theory of value, and by extension the theory of poetic value which grows out of it, contains no check against uncritical irrationalism and emotionalism. Although it would be far from what Richards intends, his principle that "experi-ence is its own justification" provides an unanswerable justifi-cation of any extreme of sadism or totalitarian power worship in conduct or of indiscriminate emotionalism in poetry.

But Richards' problems do not end here. By denying the cognitive grounds of emotive attitudes, Richards invites a hor-net's nest of problems concerning the place and function of intellectual *reference* in poetry, an issue about which he be-trays much uncertainty. On the one hand, he adheres to the view that attitudes are "self-supporting," psychologically inde-pendent of references, and he goes so far as to assert that "the emotions and attitudes resulting from a statement used emo-tively need not be directed towards anything to which the statement refers."[23] On the other hand, Richards acknowledges that references must be present if language is to evoke atti-tudes. References, he says, are usually involved as "*conditions for,* or *stages in,* the ensuing development of attitudes." "Their sole function is to bring about and support the attitudes which are the further response."[24] The two positions appear incom-

23. *Ibid.,* p. 273.
24. *Ibid.,* pp. 267–68.

patible. It is said that attitudes are "self-supporting" but that they usually require references to "support" them. The apparent contradiction may perhaps be eliminated, however, if a distinction is drawn between the meanings of "support" as the word is evidently used by Richards. References may be said to "support" attitudes in the sense that they are necessary conditions for the formation of attitudes, but not to "support" them in the sense that they *cause* attitudes or in the sense that they act as the ground for the justification of attitudes. That is, attitudes must attach themselves to references but are neither stimulated nor validated by them.

Although this distinction does seem to lessen the inconsistency, Richards nevertheless appears to be guilty of considerable vacillation and confusion over the question of reference and the referential supports of emotion. For example, he condemns "mixed modes of writing which enlist the reader's feeling as well as his thinking," and he calls for "a spell of purer science and purer poetry" as a corrective, a position which seems to eliminate even the instrumental use of references.[25] He holds that "poetry conclusively shows that even the most important among our attitudes can be aroused and maintained without any belief entering in at all."[26] But he also says that the kind of poetry for which "total independence of all beliefs is an easy matter" is "never poetry of the more important kind,"[27] and he consistently condemns other theories which turn poetry into "make-believe."[28] In *Practical Criticism* Richards condemns verse in which "a commonplace of thought or feeling . . . is delivered with an air appropriate to a fresh discovery or a revelation," implying that referential adequacy *is* a factor in the justification of attitude.[29] And in *Principles of Literary Criticism* it is more than mildly astonish-

25. *Ibid.*, p. 3.
26. *Science and Poetry*, p. 72.
27. *Ibid.*, p. 92.
28. *Principles of Literary Criticism*, p. 266.
29. *Practical Criticism* (New York: Harcourt, Brace & Co., 1935), p. 207.

ing when, after once more asserting that it is "no defect" if the referential content of a poem is "on examination, frankly false," Richards inexplicably adds: "Unless, indeed, the obviousness of the falsity forces the reader to reactions which are incongruent or disturbing to the poem."[30] Here referential falsity, previously dismissed as irrelevant to the proper development of the emotional response, is suddenly said to have the power of vitiating that response. Richards, of course, consistently maintains that people read badly, allowing empirical considerations to obtrude upon and blight their responses. But now it is implied that when the falsity of the poem is an obstacle, it may be the *poem* that is defective, not the reader!

By making emotive attitudes independent of references and by making poetic value independent of referential truth, Richards' theory guarantees its inevitable frustration, since it can give no clear or plausible explanation of the importance of reference in poetry and it cannot provide workable criteria of evaluation. Richards does not *want* to embrace irrationalism, to conflate poetry and wish fulfillment, or to cut poetry off from the real world. He insists that poetry is a means of "adjustment" to reality. Anticipating the likely objection to his view, he cautions the reader that he is not recommending a "process of pretending to ourselves that things are not as they are." The use of fictions in support of emotive beliefs, he says, is "perfectly compatible with the fullest and grimmest recognition of the exact state of affairs on all occasions. It is no make-believe."[31] But the presumably grim recognition of actuality is "compatible" with the enjoyment of emotive belief-feelings only in the sense in which two things may be said to be compatible when they have nothing to do with each other—as science is compatible with poetry. Since it is not permissible to ground one's emotional adjustment in empirical knowledge, it is difficult to see how reality can enter into the poetic experi-

30. *Principles of Literary Criticism*, p. 272.
31. *Ibid.*, p. 266.

ence at all. Richards is opposed to any theory of poetry as make-believe, yet the assumptions of his theory make it impossible for him to establish that connection between poetry and the external world which would make poetry more than make-believe.

Although Richards is certainly an extreme case, it is my view that difficulties of this sort will tend to plague any theory which denies that poetry asserts anything or refuses to recognize the relevance of referential truth and falsity. To deny that a poem asserts anything is to place the poem's intellectual content in an indeterminate position with respect to the whole, to forfeit the possibility of sufficient evaluative criteria, and to render ambiguous the relation between poetry and the real world. Moreover, to adopt the antipropositional view is to be thrown back upon a concept of emotive self-justification whose circularity and evasiveness guarantee failure. If poetic emotions cannot be grounded upon objectively asserted views of the world, they cannot be grounded upon anything. To pretend that emotions can be grounded upon themselves, that experience is its own justification, is to invite the demise of any reasonable ground for poetics.

The Later Richards

Analysts of contemporary criticism often take the view that the theories of Richards underwent a sudden and radical transformation, particularly with respect to the referential aspect of poetry, following his publications of the twenties. These commentators find it hard to explain why Richards himself not only failed to acknowledge his transformation but actually denied its having taken place. In a late essay, Richards says that, apart from changes in "vocabulary," his position remains what it was in his earlier works.[32] It is true, as Richard Foster says in his chapter on Richards in *The New Romantics*, that "changes

32. *Speculative Instruments* (Chicago: University of Chicago Press, 1955), p. 53, n. 1.

46

in language mean changes in the quality and coloration of the thought they embody—changes, that is, in 'sensibility.' "[33] But it is necessary to call into question the widespread interpretation, most recently expounded by Foster, which sees Richards' theory as having undergone a "shift away from 'positivism' " and *"toward* a condition of mind that is pretty accurately described by the word 'romanticism.' "[34] In my opinion, positivism figures no less intimately in the theory of the later Richards than in the earlier, and romanticism is as apt a term for describing the earlier work as the later.

This seeming paradox is resolved if a more scrupulous examination is undertaken of the relation between positivism and romanticism than Foster provides. Foster succeeds in demonstrating the large extent to which the New Critical view of poetry is rooted in a romantic tradition which consciously rebels against the world-view of positivism and scientific rationalism. What Foster ignores, however, and what is at present not very widely appreciated, is the fact that the romantic or new romantic view shares a number of common assumptions with the positivist-rationalist outlook it opposes.

Positivism and romanticism, despite the vast differences in style and temperament which distinguish them, share in common the assumption, discussed in Chapter One, that intellectually formulable or rational knowledge is strictly limited to quantifiable fact and that reason has no access to the realm of values. Logical positivism, although customarily thought of as trumpeting the power of reason, actually enforces a stringent narrowing of the scope of reason. The romantic, though he protests the positivist's devaluation of metaphysics and the imagination, accepts implicitly the premises on which the devaluation is grounded—the impotence of reason in the realm of values. Thus it is that the positivist and the romantic collaborate in erecting a barrier between science, logic, and rational

33. *The New Romantics* (Bloomington: Indiana University Press, 1962), p. 61.
34. *Ibid.,* p. 47.

modes of communication on the one hand, and myth and the language of imagination, value judgment, and emotion on the other. Positivist and romantic alike, although moved by antithetical interests, join in separating poetry from empirically verifiable statement. It may be hazarded that the romantic is often, perhaps always, an inverted positivist—an extreme skeptic with regard to the powers of reason and logic, albeit with a complementary faith in the validity of nonrational modes of thought.

Robert Langbaum, in *The Poetry of Experience*, argues that "Romanticism is . . . not so much a reaction against eighteenth-century empiricism as a reaction within it."[35] As Langbaum suggests, it is significant that Wordsworth's discovery of his creative and imaginative powers in *The Prelude* takes place only after his earlier rationalism has led him to become skeptical toward the rational mind: "Wearied out with contraries," he says he "yielded up moral questions in despair." Having rejected the possibility that reason may have any efficacy in determining values, Wordsworth, and the positivist-romantic generally, is faced with the problem of recovering and rehabilitating emotion and action, of finding a ground for response in lieu of objective, rational knowledge. This is the problem experienced by Mill in his *Autobiography*, when, suffering the corrosive effects of his "analytic habits," he finds himself unable any longer to feel. It is the problem experienced by Carlyle's Teufelsdröckh in *Sartor Resartus*, when his youthful rationalism brings him to a vision of the universe as "one huge, dead, immeasurable Steam-engine, rolling on, in its dead indifference, to grind me limb from limb"—the Everlasting No.

In each of these instances, the skeptical and positivistic assumption that reason functions only in the realm of quantifiable fact is a necessary precondition of the subsequent affirmation of the romantic creative imagination as a new ground of

35. *The Poetry of Experience* (New York: Random House, 1957), p. 22.

value and response. In each instance, in other words, the romantic affirmation is based upon a positivistic definition of the terms of the problem. Reason must be defined as morally bankrupt; the boundaries between reason and imagination, science and poetry, must be drawn so as to exclude each other.

This positivist-romantic pattern is illustrated in the poetic theory of the early Richards. Richards' view that emotive response cannot be grounded upon knowledge or belief is his positivistic Everlasting No, his seeming denial of the possibility of value. But the notion that, "having cut our pseudo-statements free from belief," we can still retain them in a "released state, as the main instruments by which we order our attitudes to one another and the world," a notion fortified by the principle that "experience is its own justification," constitutes his romantic affirmation, his Everlasting Yea. Again, the romantic affirmation presupposes the positivistic negation.[36]

36. The closeness of Richards' position to traditional romantic attitudes is reflected in the presence in his criticism of deliberate echoes of certain familiar romantic poems. For instance, compare his comment that poetry seems "to lift away the burden of existence" so that "we seem ourselves to be looking into the heart of things" (*Principles of Literary Criticism*, p. 283) with the lines in "Tintern Abbey" which it paraphrases. Of course Richards regards Wordsworth's celebration of a pantheistic Spirit of Nature in that poem as an emotive attitude only—we only "seem" to be relieved of "the weary weight of all this unintelligible world" and only seem to see into the life of things. But the poem's argument and Richards' psychological theory of value are informed by similar sentimentalist or pragmatic premises, namely, that "the justification of any attitude *per se* is its success for the needs of the being," and not "the soundness of the views which may seem to be . . . its ground and causes." When Wordsworth writes:

> If this
> Be but a vain belief, yet oh! how oft—
> In darkness and amid the many shapes
> Of joyless daylight; when the fretful stir
> Unprofitable, and the fever of the world,
> Have hung upon the beatings of my heart—
> How oft, in spirit have I turned to thee,
> O sylvan Wye!

he says, in effect, that even in the event his belief in nature's healing power should be a delusion, it is worth maintaining anyway, since it satisfies "the needs of the being." Even if it is not true, it is congenial, and this is what matters. In view of such passages as this it is odd to find Richards scolding Wordsworth for taking his pantheistic notions seri-

In a similar manner, the conception of poetry held by the New Critics and the mythopoeic critics—poetry as a dramatic embodiment of nonlogical, imaginative knowledge—depends upon and presupposes a positivistic conception of the limitations of reason. The fact that these theorists tend to think of themselves as antipositivistic only betrays a certain lack of self-knowledge on their part. If one fails to see the similarity of romantic and positivistic assumptions, one cannot explain the fact that such opponents of positivism as Tate, Wimsatt, and Wheelwright base their own theories upon dualisms of scientific and poetic discourse which are strikingly like those of Richards and the positivists.

Those who have popularized the theory of the later Richards' conversion are literary critics who were dismayed by the positivism of the early works, and who applaud in the later works what they take to be a more congenial attitude toward truth and knowledge as constituents of poetry. The general contention of these interpreters is that in *Coleridge on Imagination* (1934) and his subsequent works, Richards repudiated his earlier positivist view of poetry as pseudo-statement and came to see poetry as a special kind of truth and knowledge, that "unique mode of knowing" so often celebrated—if not defined—by the later New Critics and others. Richard Foster says:

> The earlier Richards would surely have objected . . . to the later Richards' defense of Coleridge's vitalist view of "the mind" as preferable to the mechanist view. Coleridge's "conception of the mind as an active, self-forming, self-realizing system," wrote the later Richards, "is plainly an immense improvement."[37]

Here, Foster suggests, Richards is seen in the act of repudiating mechanistic thinking in general. But if the statements quoted

ously as if they were scientific truths instead of being content to enjoy them as pure emotive gratifications (*Principles of Literary Criticism*, pp. 274–75).

37. *New Romantics*, p. 54.

by Foster are read in the context of Richards' argument in *Coleridge on Imagination*, it turns out that he is holding up Coleridge's vitalism as "an immense improvement" not over "the mechanist view," as Foster says, but over "*theories of association*, by which a state of mind is represented as a cluster . . . of revived impressions fished up from a mental storehouse . . ."[38] Richards is actually objecting not to mechanist views in general but to those of the associationist variety. He continues to identify himself with mechanist views: "I write . . . as a Materialist trying to interpret . . . the utterances of an extreme Idealist."[39] What Foster assumes to be evidence of a change of mind is simply one more expression of Richards' long-standing dislike of associationist theories of psychology and language, a dislike which is stated unequivocally in both *The Meaning of Meaning* (1923) ("The doctrines of the associationists . . . tend to separate the treatment of fundamental laws of mental process from that of sign-interpretation, which is unfortunate for psychology."[40]) and in *Principles of Literary Criticism* (1924) ("The old associationists supposed the records to be writ small inside separate cells. The more modern view was that they were scored large through a deepening of the channels of conduction. Neither view is adequate."[41]). It is only by removing Richards' statements from their context that they can be interpreted as marking a change in thinking.

The passage that is most frequently cited, however, to support the claim that Richards reversed his position is the following from *The Philosophy of Rhetoric* (1936):

So far from verbal language being a "compromise for a language of intuition"—a thin, but better-than-nothing substitute for real experience,—language, well used, is a *comple-*

38. *Coleridge on Imagination* (New York: W. W. Norton & Co., 1950), p. 69 (italics added).
39. *Ibid.*, p. 19.
40. I. A. Richards and C. K. Ogden, *The Meaning of Meaning* (New York: Harcourt, Brace & Co., 1938), p. 51.
41. *Principles of Literary Criticism*, p. 104.

tion and does what the intuitions of sensation by themselves cannot do. Words are the meeting points at which regions of experience which can never combine in sensation or intuition, come together. They are the occasion and the means of that growth which is the mind's endless endeavour to order itself. That is why we have language. It is no mere signalling system. It is the instrument of all our distinctively human development, of everything in which we go beyond the other animals.[42]

Here again, if the interpreters are correct, is the essence of the New Richards, emancipated at last from his positivist bondage. As Allen Tate puts it, "There is, in this passage, . . . an implicit repudiation of the leading doctrine of *The Principles of Literary Criticism* [*sic*]. The early doctrine did look upon poetic language as a 'substitute for real experience,' if by experience is meant responses relevant to scientifically ascertained facts and situations." Tate adds: "Language, says Mr. Richards, 'is no mere signalling system.' With that sentence the early psychological doctrine is discretely put away."[43] Tate further interprets Richards' disparagement of "sensation" and "intuition" in the passage as an implicit repudiation of the behaviorist approach to language interpretation. Foster also quotes the passage and echoes Tate's remarks.

But a look at the text reveals again that the repudiations are in the eye of the beholder. The passage comes as an extended critique of associationists, who reduce poetry to concrete imagery and visualizable mental pictures. The objection to the view of language as a "compromise for a language of intuition" is an objection not to the behavioristic interpretation of language but to the theory of T. E. Hulme, from whom the phrase is quoted. It is Hulme and his followers, not the earlier Richards nor the behaviorists, whom Richards is accusing of

42. *The Philosophy of Rhetoric* (New York: Oxford University Press, 1936), pp. 130-31.
43. *The Man of Letters in the Modern World* (New York: Meridian Books, 1955), pp. 59-60.

turning language into a mere "signalling system." The paragraph from which the passage is taken begins as a protest against the "blunder" of teachers who attempt to "make children visualize where visualization is a mere distraction and of no service." Richards is attacking only that tendency which, as we have seen above, he had attacked many times in his books of ten years earlier—the associationist concept of the mind as a "storehouse" of images. This is what he is opposing when he asserts that language is not a "substitute for real experience." Again, there is ample precedent in the earlier writings: in *Principles of Literary Criticism* he says that "too much importance has always been attached to the sensory qualities of images," and he goes on to argue that an image is a "representative of a sensation," a "mental event peculiarly connected with a sensation," whose effect depends upon this fact rather than on any supposed "sensory resemblance" to a sensation.[44] And in *Practical Criticism* (1929) he repeats his protest against the "confusion" of attributing the effects of images to visualization.[45] Again, by simply paying no attention to the context, the interpreters have transformed a familiar and characteristic protest against associationism into a sardonic commentary on the early works.

But what of Tate's remark that the early Richards saw poetic language as "a substitute for real experience"? Tate goes on to say that although poetry for the early Richards was supposedly "the orderer of our minds . . . the valuer, . . . the ordering mysteriously operated in fictions irrelevant to the real world."[46] Tate offers a reasonable criticism here—in fact, my own observations earlier in this chapter echo his—but there is still no reason to suppose that Richards has reversed his position. When the later Richards says that words are the "meeting points" at which experiences come together, is there any reason to believe he has something different in mind than he had

44. *Principles of Literary Criticism*, pp. 119–20.
45. *Practical Criticism*, pp. 362–64.
46. *Man of Letters in the Modern World*, p. 60.

earlier when he claimed that the pseudo-statement is the main instrument "by which we order our attitudes to one another and to the world," that it is "no make-believe"? Richards insisted from the beginning that poetry and the external world are related, but he never succeeded in making clear what that relationship is. We have no warrant for supposing a reversal when he asserts once more that a relationship exists.

In *Coleridge on Imagination*, Richards constructs a "derived instrument," partly of Coleridge's invention, partly of his own, amounting to a theory of the creative imagination and of the nature of poetry. At the basis of this theory is a "projective-realist synthesis"—a reconciliation of the "realist doctrine," that the subject perceives an objective reality in nature, with the "projective doctrine," that what the subject perceives is a projection of its own feelings, aspirations, and apprehensions.[47] Through this reconciliation, Richards hopes to achieve a marriage of his own materialism with Coleridge's idealism, thus resolving the traditional problem of romantic aesthetics—the resolution of the internal, contextual autonomy of the subjective experience of the poem with the referential, objective, and normative claims of the poem. Richards will then have resolved the central antinomy of modern poetics, which, as we saw in Chapter One, Coleridge himself was able to resolve only by appeal to the transcendental mystery of the Spirit of Nature.[48]

Richards' synthesis of the projective and realist doctrines is based upon the argument that these doctrines, mutually contradictory though they may appear, are not "necessarily in opposition to one another" and that they are—"in the only interpretations in which either is true—both true."[49] But what does Richards mean by the qualification, "in the only interpretations in which either is true"? Here we find Richards' con-

47. *Coleridge on Imagination*, p. 145.
48. See above, pp. 18–19.
49. *Coleridge on Imagination*, p. 146.

tinued dependence upon the positivist cleavage between empirical and metaphysical statements. For what Richards has in mind is the idea that propositions which do not assert anything about verifiable states of affairs cannot conflict with other propositions or with each other. Richards compares the two statements, "A man is an immortal spirit" and "Water freezes at 32° F.," and he observes, "In the senses in which we will agree that the second . . . [is] true, it would be *nonsense* to say that the first is."[50] The first statement, since no amount of empirical evidence brought to bear on it can determine its truth or falsity, is "nonsense" in the positivist's sense—a pseudo-statement which asserts nothing. Whatever "truth" it may be said to have will be a truth beyond experience, different in kind from the truth of the second statement. But because of this fact, the first statement is incapable of conflicting with other statements. One may legitimately extend Richards' illustration by pointing out that, in the context of his argument, the statements, "A man is an immortal spirit" and "A man is *not* an immortal spirit" are, in the only interpretations in which either is true, both true. Since pseudo-statements cannot conflict, the identity of spirit and matter is confirmed.

Since the projective and realist epistemological doctrines are empirically untestable, they are both pseudo-statements and hence subject to the same "interpretations" extended to the paradigm statement about immortality. Thus the truth of these doctrines is a truth of precisely the same kind:

> Similarly with the two doctrines I am here considering. They are neither consequences of *a priori* decisions, nor verifiable as the empirical statements of the sciences are verifiable; and all verifiable statements are independent of them. But this does not diminish in the least their interest, or that of the other senses in which they may be said to be true.[51]

50. *Ibid.*, p. 147.
51. *Ibid.*, pp. 147–48.

The "truth," then, to which Richards' synthesis of Coleridgean idealism and Ricardian materialism appeals, is nothing more than the quasi-hypothetical kind which the positivist condescends to permit so long as it is relegated to the other side of the border separating certifiable empirical propositions from pseudo-propositions which may be true only because they can never be shown to be false. This is a truth by default, a truth conditional upon the impossibility of any appeal to objective experience.

But this is but another way of saying what Richards himself surely would not deny—that the "truth" he is here invoking is indistinguishable from emotional satisfaction or what the earlier Richards called "emotive belief." The projective and realist doctrines, Richards points out, are most profitably viewed not as "doctrines" at all but as "imaginative acts" or, in Coleridge's phrase, "facts of mind." That these "facts of mind" are identical with what Richards previously called emotive beliefs is indicated by the fact that Richards consistently opposes them to doctrines and intellectual formulations, that is, to scientific statements:

> The difficulty of this study is in preventing our attention straying from utterances as facts of mind to something else —the supposed states of affairs which we take them to be utterances about. To say something, to represent some supposed state of affairs, is *one* function of language—an important but not exclusive function.[52]

Richards' continued reliance upon the concept of the dual functions of language is obvious in this statement. The projective-realist synthesis is a "fact of mind," and its expression in language is an emotive utterance in the sense defined by the early Richards. It remains solidly within the class of utterances whose function is to express attitudes, not to point accurately to the objective world.

52. *Ibid.*, p. 143.

But what of Richards' use of the word "truth" throughout this discussion? Foster says that the earlier Richards "would not be able to imagine what other senses of *true* might exist outside the defining principle of at least theoretical verifiability," and that Richards would earlier have protested against the misuse of the word as applied to the special kind of "knowledge" accorded to facts of mind and poetic myths in *Coleridge on Imagination.*[53] This is simply false. In *The Meaning of Meaning* Richards and Ogden distinguish between "True^S" as applied to "symbolic"—i.e., empirical—statements and "True^E" as applied to emotive utterances: "Critics often use True^E of works of art, where alternative symbols would be 'convincing' in some cases, 'sincere' in others, 'beautiful' in others, and so on."[54] The authors go on to complain that this is too often done "without any awareness that True^E and True^S are different symbols"; but this is an objection not to the legitimacy of the application of "true" to emotive utterances and poetry, but to the confusion of the emotive sense of the word with the scientific sense, a distinction which Richards has emphasized throughout his work. The earlier Richards not only *would* have accepted the later Richards' use of "true" "outside the defining principle of . . . verifiability," but *did* accept it.

Richards' synthesis of his own materialism with Coleridge's idealism according to the principle that emotive statements cannot conflict is foreshadowed at several points in his earlier works. The following passage from *Principles of Literary Criticism* contains the essence of the argument in *Coleridge on Imagination:*

53. *New Romantics,* p. 58.
54. *Meaning of Meaning,* p. 151. More recently, Richards has proposed the word "troth" to describe emotive commitments, expressions of faith, loyalty, etc. (*Speculative Instruments,* pp. 140–41, 177–78). See also "Emotive Language Still," *Yale Review,* XXXIX (Autumn, 1949), 108–18. "Troth" is obviously a synonym for "Truth^E"; this further testifies to the continuation of the positivist-emotivist position in the later writings.

The view that we are our bodies, more especially our nervous systems, more especially still the higher or central co-ordinating parts of it, and that the mind is a system of impulses should not be described as Materialism. It might equally well be called Idealism. Neither term in this connection has any scientific, any strictly symbolic meaning or reference. Neither stands for any separable, observable group of things. Each is primarily an emotive term used to incite or support certain emotional attitudes. Like all terms used in the vain attempt (vain, because the question is nonsensical) to say what things are, instead of to say how they behave, they state nothing.[55]

The view of the universe as a machine and the view of it as a living organism are not really in opposition, since neither view really asserts anything. As Richards goes on to say, the fact that the materialist and idealist believe themselves to be holding incompatible views is merely an instance of "the widespread confusion between scientific statement and emotive appeal." "The Mind-Body problem is strictly speaking no problem; it is an *imbroglio* due to failure to settle a real problem, namely as to when we are making a statement and when merely inciting an attitude."[56] The warning corresponds exactly to that made in *Coleridge on Imagination* to the effect that we must distinguish between "utterances as facts of mind" and statements which "represent some supposed states of affairs," lest we confuse emotive attitudes with scientific statements.

In Chapter One, I observed that Coleridge's theory of the creative imagination depends upon the transcendentalist doctrine of the Spirit of Nature, admittedly a mystery, as the only way of reconciling the conflicting claims of idealism and realism, of subjective autonomy and objective truth, order, and value. The Spirit of Nature, infusing both subject and object, reconciles all contraries into a higher unity. Whereas Coleridge invoked a transcendentalist spiritualism in order to assert that

55. *Principles of Literary Criticism*, pp. 83–84.
56. *Ibid.*

the imagination yields truth, Richards invokes a materialistic positivism in order to assert that the imagination can never be false. The knowledge which Richards' theory attributes to poetry and myth is a knowledge which can be safely ascribed only because it can never be verified or falsified, a knowledge compounded of the emotive preferences of the materialist and idealist, neither of which has any ground in objective reality. Such is the "unique mode of knowing" which the later Richards has been thought to have ascribed to poetry.

Ingenious though it may be, Richards' argument presents nothing new in the way of a solution to the problems discussed in the first part of this chapter. Since the truth of poetic myth is admittedly still no more than emotive satisfaction, no new basis for poetic response has been established. In basing our emotions upon the mythologies of the imagination, we are doing precisely what Richards had urged in his early works—basing our emotions upon themselves. In no sense have the myths of poetry been brought into closer relation with the objective world. Poetry is to be as "independent" of real knowledge as it ever was.

It is worth noting that if Richards' projective-realist synthesis, and the theory of imagination and poetry derived from it, is admittedly no more than a pseudo-statement, then poetic theory has itself become a kind of poetry. This is precisely the thesis which Foster's *The New Romantics* has developed with respect to the New Critics generally, whose essays are frequently a kind of "secondary protective poetry." But surely, it will be objected, the earlier Richards' emphasis on scientific analysis and classification is far from the sort of critical poetizing described by Foster. After all, does not Richards call the theory outlined in *Principles of Literary Criticism* "a machine to think with," in contrast to *Coleridge on Imagination*, which is dominated by the organic analogy?

It is easy to be misled here, particularly if too much importance is assigned to the scientific paraphernalia of the early works, the neurological charts and diagrams, the technical vocabulary, the quantitative and experimental approach to values. These may cause one to overlook the fact that beneath the scientific trappings lies a theory which contains in itself an implicit denial of the possibility of an objective approach to poetry. For it must be remembered that for Richards normative judgments are subsumed under psychology—values are simply emotive satisfactions. It follows that statements expressing value judgments, including the valuations of criticism, although they may be analyzed scientifically, cannot be rationally grounded—they are acts of pure emotive preference. For Richards, critical choices are "spontaneous" and "irreflective";[57] they are prior to reflection, the purely emotive preference itself being all the justification it requires—indeed, all it can possibly have in a world in which experience is its own justification. To base critical judgments upon "principles" would be to base emotions upon intellectual grounds external to the emotions, a procedure which Richards regards as psychological perversion. The theory set down in *Principles of Literary Criticism* represents an implicit denial of the validity of principles.

Hence Richards' frequently noted tendency in his later works to eschew the elaborate technical machinery in favor of a more openly emotive approach is not really very surprising, given the extreme anti-intellectualist implications of the early theory itself. Such analytical machinery had no real justification in the theory anyway, except insofar as it might provide information about our responses which we do not need to know, the proper development of response being prior to, and independent of, its explanations. In fact there would appear to be a very serious contradiction inherent in Richards' very effort to promote understanding of the poetic response, since according to his premises such understanding can only frustrate and corrupt response. The more overt indulgence in an

57. *Ibid.*, p. 198.

emotive stance of the later Richards represents not a reversal of the earlier position but a logical outcome of that position.

Allen Tate says that Richards' intellectual history "will probably turn out to be the most instructive, among critics, of our age."[58] If that is true, it ought not to be for the reasons Tate has in mind. The theory of the later Richards is a restatement of the positivist-romantic position of which the earlier works are the definitive formulation. To see the later Richards as having repudiated his earlier view of poetry in favor of a theory which confronts the problem of poetry and knowledge in a new and more adequate way is to argue not only against the testimony of Richards himself but against the evidence as well.[59]

The Collapse of Traditional Poetics

In construing as a form of "psychological perversion" the model of response in which emotions derive their justification with reference to their cognitive grounds, Richards' theory may be taken to represent an advanced stage in the history of the collapse of traditional poetics. Richards' theory of the independence of emotive attitudes from referential grounds is symptomatic of the breakdown of the traditional ground-consequent scheme which, from antiquity through much of the eighteenth century, governed poetics by providing a model for the relationship of cognitive understanding and emotional response. The concept of a "rationally grounded" or "just" emotional response, which sounds so foreign to modern ears, formed the basis of the classical theory of poetic decorum. Plato, although he denigrated poetry in Book X of the *Re-*

---

58. *Man of Letters in the Modern World*, p. 59.
59. For a detailed discussion of the relationship of the early and later Richards, see Jerome P. Schiller, *I. A. Richards' Theory of Literature* (New Haven: Yale University Press, 1969), pp. 3–18 and *passim*. Schiller does not devote much attention, however, to the issue of poetic truth.

public, established in the process the terms upon which the defense of poetry would rest for centuries. For Plato, emotional responses, and their formal correlatives in verbal style and rhythm, ought to be "appropriate to a life of courage and self-control." Poetic form is not arbitrary decoration but reflects a moral posture toward experience: "metre and music must be adapted to the sense of the words," and "the content of the poetry and the manner in which it is expressed depend, in their turn, on moral character." Plato does not banish all poetry from his ideal state but exempts the kind "which will fittingly represent the tones and accents of a brave man in warlike action or in any hard and dangerous task, who, in the hour of defeat or when facing wounds and death, will meet every blow of fortune with steadfast endurance," the kind which "will best express the accents of courage in the face of stern necessity." In other words, a proper style will reflect those emotions which possess an intimate connection with philosophic wisdom and ethical maturity. Conversely, the crude and insensitive style tends to reflect an inadequate understanding and response: "the absense of grace, rhythm, harmony is nearly allied to baseness of thought and expression and baseness of character."[60] Soundness of style reflects a soundness of emotional attitude which in turn reflects a soundness of intellectual understanding.

This principle of decorum, applied with much greater flexibility with respect to what constitutes an acceptable response than Plato would have permitted, remains intact from antiquity through the Renaissance. Sidney, in the *Defense of Poesy* asserts the principle when he says that the poet must weigh "each syllable of each word by just proportion, according to the dignity of the subject."[61] In the eighteenth century, despite the counterinfluence of Dr. Johnson, the old understanding of

60. *The Republic of Plato,* ed. and trans. F. M. Cornford (New York: Oxford University Press, 1945), pp. 87–90.

61. *The Defense of Poesy,* ed. Albert S. Cook (Boston: Ginn and Co., 1890), p. 11. See below, Chapter Six, pp. 161–66, and Appendix B.

the relationship between conceptual subject and feeling begins to weaken, and there arises on the one hand the frequently debased and shallow conception of reason found in neoclassical theory, and on the other hand the cult of the sublime, which tends to elevate the emotions associated with sublimity apart from the rational understanding of the objects which occasion them. But it is not until the nineteenth century that poetic emotions are decisively disengaged from objective understanding of subject matter. Although rational truth is still sometimes accorded an honorable place in poetry, as in the ambivalent Coleridge, many theorists assign reason a subordinate status. As M. H. Abrams notes, in such theorists as John Stuart Mill and Alexander Smith, subject matter and propositional meaning are seen as mere pretexts or convenient props, useful in facilitating emotion but of no importance in themselves.[62] For Smith, "in poetry, . . . the information furnished is merely subsidiary to the conveyance of the emotion."[63] Gerard Manley Hopkins sums up this view later in the century when he writes in his notebook that "some matter and meaning is essential but only as an element necessary to support and employ the shape which is contemplated for its own sake."[64] Edgar Allan Poe, in a formulation which anticipates Richards, says that "the precepts of Duty, or even the lessons of Truth" may be introduced into a poem, but only on the condition that they "subserve incidentally . . . the general purposes of the work," purposes which Poe sees as having nothing to do with truth or duty.[65] If "the attainment of a truth" helps us "to perceive a harmony where none was apparent before," then the success of this "true poetical effect" is "referable to the harmony alone,

62. *The Mirror and the Lamp: Romantic Theory and the Critical Tradition* (New York: Oxford University Press, 1953), pp. 322–24. Abrams calls attention to the similarity of these views with Richards' theory of pseudo-statements.

63. Quoted by Abrams, *ibid.*, p. 322.

64. *The Note-books and Papers of G. M. Hopkins,* ed. Humphrey House (New York: Oxford University Press, 1937), pp. 249–51.

65. "The Poetic Principle," in *Selected Poetry and Prose,* ed. T. O. Mabbott (New York: Random House, 1951), p. 390.

and not in the least degree to the truth which merely served to render the harmony manifest."[66] This clearly anticipates Richards' pragmatic theory of poetic response as an emotive "sense" of harmony, "supported" by references but independent of truth. Poe goes on to commend the versification of a poem as "admirably adapted to the wild insanity which is the thesis of the poem,"[67] here invoking in a naïve form the "principle of dramatic propriety" subsequently to be developed by Cleanth Brooks.[68] In Poe, style remains—as it was in Plato—a reflection of emotional attitudes; however, it is judged not with reference to the poet's philosophic understanding of his subject and the ethical validity of his response but reflexively, with reference only to the emotional attitude itself—the state of mind of the speaker of the poem. The emotional attitude—in this instance "wild insanity"—has become its own justification, requiring no ground in predicated understanding.

Thus we arrive at that process of doubling back upon themselves which the emotions are forced to undergo when the intellect is narrowed to the province of scientific neutrality and the ground-consequent relationship between conceptual predication and emotion is destroyed. From this destruction issue the dilemmas of circularity, subjectivism, and relativism in which romantic and modernist aesthetics are trapped. The later theories of mythopoeic critics and New Critical organicists, to be examined in the next two chapters, arise out of the same dilemma, and these theories propose analogous theories of autonomy, beset by analogous difficulties, in response to it.

66. *Ibid.*, p. 399.
67. *Ibid.*, p. 402.
68. See below, pp. 94–103.

CHAPTER THREE

Mythopoeic Criticism:
The Visionary Imagination

On the surface, it might seem that Richards' hard-headed positivistic realism bears slight resemblance to the idealism which pervades the thinking of such influential proponents of the mythopoeic approach to poetry as Ernst Cassirer and C. G. Jung. Richards dismisses the preoccupations of the Jungian school as superstition,[1] and, despite his fascination with Coleridge, he does not embrace the neo-Kantian epistemology of the philosophers of symbolic forms, for whom language is constitutive of reality. Cassirer's treatment of poetry as an objectification of prelogical, mythic consciousness and its peculiar laws finds no clear analogy in Richards, who refuses to acknowledge the existence of any distinct logic, or paralogic, of the poetic mind. Whereas Cassirer endorses the Kantian principle of the disinterestedness of aesthetic experience, Richards, the Benthamite, proclaims the utility of the arts and the continuity of aesthetic and nonaesthetic experience.

On the other hand, if we look further, we find certain

1. *Principles of Literary Criticism* (New York: Harcourt, Brace & World, 1928), p. 281.

important similarities. We have seen that Richards views values as projections of emotive needs upon the dead and "neutralised" phenomena of nature; in this he is not far from Cassirer, Jung, and such later mythopoeic critics as Northrop Frye, for whom values are man-made constructions imposed upon a nature which is meaningless—"dead, cold and unending" in Jung's phrase[2]—apart from man's imaginative shaping of it. As we shall see in the present chapter, this metaphysical orientation on the part of the mythopoeic critics whose theories we shall be examining leads them to define poetry in terms essentially similar to those of the Ricardian pseudo-statement.

Cassirer, Langer, Jung

For Ernst Cassirer, the subjectivity of the mythic consciousness, where poetry originates, is no obstacle to the formulation of the criteria which govern its characteristic modes of thought. The forms of mythical thought, Cassirer argues, make up a coherent, highly organized, and self-contained world, the laws of which are independent of empirical truth and discursive logic. Hence, "instead of measuring the content, meaning, and truth of intellectual forms by something extraneous which is supposed to be reproduced in them, we must find in these forms themselves the measure and criterion for their truth and intrinsic meaning."[3] Of course for Cassirer, science and "theoretical thought" are themselves symbolic forms, whose "objectivity" and truth derive not from a correspondence to some "extraneous" *Ding an sich* but from a consistency with the internally established laws of theoretical thought itself. For theoretical thought, "the criterion for truth and objectivity . . . is the factor of permanence, of logical constancy, and logical necessity." Science dissects "the simple matter of sen-

2. *Symbols of Transformation*, trans. by F. C. Hull (New York: Harper Brothers, 1956), I, 25.
3. *Language and Myth*, trans. Susanne Langer (New York: Dover Publications, 1946), p. 8.

sory impressions into strata of 'grounds' and 'consequences,'"
referring everything to the principle of sufficient reason as its
"supreme postulate." In that sense this kind of thought submits
the objects of its reflection to "extraneous" measurement.
"Such a differentiation and stratification is totally alien to the
mythical consciousness," however. "This consciousness lives in
the immediate impression, which it accepts without measuring
it by something else." "Each object that engages and fills the
mythical consciousness pertains, as it were, only to itself."[4]

In the second volume of his *Philosophy of Symbolic Forms*,
and in brief outline in his *Essay on Man*, Cassirer develops his
"critical phenomenology of the mythical consciousness."[5] The
categories of mythic thought are said to be the same as those of
theoretic thought—space, time, relation, cause, etc.—but their
"modality" differs. For example, with regard to *relation*, both
the mythical and scientific outlooks possess a concept of unity,
but whereas the scientific consciousness perceives a "synthetic
unity, a unity of *different* entities," in the mythical realm there
is "but one dimension of relation, one single 'plane of being.'"[6]
A "law of metamorphosis" obtains whereby everything potentially *is* everything else.[7] Life is not divided into classes and
subclasses but "is felt as an unbroken continuous whole which
does not admit of any clean-cut and trenchant distinctions."[8]
Everything is "real" for the mythic consciousness, and there
are no degrees of reality. The part does not "stand for" the
whole, it *is* the whole; the symbol *is* the object, not a mere
abstract representation of it; there is no distinction between
wish and fulfillment, nor between life and death. Indeed, there
is no such thing as death in mythical thought, the very idea of
separation having been obliterated by the deeper feeling "of a

4. *The Philosophy of Symbolic Forms*, trans. Ralph Manheim (New
Haven: Yale University Press, 1955), II, 73–74.
5. *Ibid.*, p. 13; *Essay on Man* (New Haven: Yale University Press,
1944).
6. *Philosophy of Symbolic Forms*, II, 63.
7. *Essay on Man*, p. 81.
8. *Ibid.*

fundamental and indelible *solidarity of life.*"[9] For the mytho-poeic critic, these characteristics of mythic thought are operative in poetry and differentiate poetry from analytic modes of discourse.

Cassirer's theory encounters difficulties which are endemic to critical arguments based upon Kantian or Neo-Kantian epistemological premises. For Cassirer language cannot be viewed as a commentary upon objective reality since language is itself "constitutive" of reality. But when the demarcation between language and reality is destroyed, the concepts of verbal truth and falsity become ambiguous and insecure. It is no longer clear why all linguistic expressions, particularly those in the mythic realm, should not be equally true and valid. Analytic thought is testable according to fixed principles which, even if they too are subjective constructions for Cassirer, are at least subject to critical validation. There are ways of determining that one analytic construction is more adequate than another. Mythical expressions, because they obey no law but that of subjective association, are not liable to similar check. Since "everything potentially *is* everything else," theoretically there is no case in which the critic can legitimately object that some comparison is forced, that some item is incongruous, that some attitude or idea is childish or fatuous. There can be no appeal to a principle of consistency since everything is "consistent" with everything. There can be no appeal to "the way things are" in experience, for that, of course, would be to judge from without. The principle of contextual independence which Cassirer accords to mythical expressions elevates them effectively beyond all criticism. This inability to specify any possible conditions for error within the "autonomous" context, leading to the perpetration of endless tautologies in critical theory, plagues all theories which ascribe to poetry a self-validating, independent contextual principle.

Cassirer does not wish to succumb to the romantic fallacy

9. *Ibid.*, p. 82.

that poetry is a raw, primitive outpouring of emotion or the unadulterated expression of hallucination and delusion. He emphasizes the process of objectification, through which emotion is given "definite shape" and a "clear organization and articulation."[10] A lyric poet, he says, is "not just a man who indulges in displays of feeling. To be swayed by emotion alone is sentimentality, not art."[11] Art, on the contrary, involves "an objective view of things and of human life"; it is a "discovery of reality."[12] But Cassirer's apparent commitment to the objective function of art is weakened by his refusal to permit abstract mediation in art. "Science," as opposed to art, "means abstraction, and abstraction is always an impoverishment of reality."[13] Art is "an interpretation of reality—not by concepts but by intuitions; not through the medium of thought but through that of sensuous forms."[14] The difficulty here is in conceiving how anything can be an "interpretation" of reality without in some way involving abstractions, "the medium of thought." With respect to verbal art at any rate, the irreducibly conceptual and mediate character of language insures that interpretations can issue out of the presentation of "sensuous forms" only when these forms are integrated into a conceptual scheme. Interpretation presupposes abstraction, the abridgement of immediacy and intuition by a conceptual framework of ideas. To banish abstraction from poetry on the assumption that sensuous immediacies can somehow convey interpretations apart from the conceptualizations they imply is to go a long way toward emptying poetry of meaning and turning the poet into "just a man who indulges in displays of feeling." And, in fact, Cassirer often speaks of poetry as a "realm of pure feeling" whose truth has nothing to do with objective reality.[15] He says that art aims at "a new kind of truth—a truth not of

10. *Ibid.*, p. 167.
11. *Ibid.*, p. 142.
12. *Ibid.*, p. 143.
13. *Ibid.*, p. 144.
14. *Ibid.*, p. 146.
15. *Language and Myth*, p. 99.

empirical things but of pure forms."[16] Art and poetry have "a purely *immanent* validity and truth." Art "does not aim at something else or refer to something else; it simply 'is' and consists in itself."[17] Such observations do little to clarify the nature of artistic and poetic truth. Although it may be unjust to accuse so distinguished a champion of rational thought of holding an anti-intellectual theory of poetry, the fact is that Cassirer's theory tends to allow no place for intellectual content and thus turns poetry into a vehicle of uncritical emotion.

This tendency appears even more noticeably in the theory of Cassirer's pupil and translator, Susanne Langer, whose concept of the nondiscursive "use" of discursive language was criticized in the last chapter.[18] Mrs. Langer adopts the conventional dichotomy of informational vs. poetic or "presentational" symbolism. Her theory of the "import" of the arts—not to be confused with the kind of meaning which conveys "something beyond itself"[19]—resembles Cassirer's concept of "immanent" validity and truth. Poetry "does not express any proposition and therefore does not advocate or confess anything."[20] The awkwardness of this position becomes especially apparent in Mrs. Langer's attempts to subsume poetic meaning under music: "The import of artistic expression is broadly the same in all arts as it is in music—the verbally ineffable, yet not inexpressible law of vital experience, the pattern of affective and sentient being."[21] Although poetry employs words and sentences instead of pure sounds, it achieves the same kind of import as music. For "the material of poetry is discursive, but the product—the artistic phenomenon—is not."[22] Whatever

16. *Essay on Man*, p. 164.
17. *Philosophy of Symbolic Forms*, II, 25–26.
18. See above, pp. 38–41.
19. *Problems of Art* (New York: Charles Scribner's Sons, 1957), p. 139.
20. *Feeling and Form* (New York: Charles Scribner's Sons, 1953), p. 257.
21. *Philosophy in a New Key*, 2d ed. (New York: New American Library, 1961), p. 217.
22. *Ibid.*, p. 221.

generalizations a poem may contain refer to no objective reality but serve to create "a virtual event," an "illusion of directly experienced life."[23] Poetry provides not moral illumination but "the illusion of a moral illumination," the immediate emotional state accompanying moral illumination. "The fixation of belief is not the poet's purpose; his purpose is the creation of a virtual experience of belief or its attainment." Argumentation in poetry is "the semblance of thought process," and the "sense of sudden revelation" which results is more important than the content of the revelation itself.[24] Such a view plainly echoes Richards' view that poetry gives a "feeling of revealed significance" without actual revelation, and it is founded upon a similar process of amputation, whereby the conceptual grounds of poetic emotions are severed from the emotions themselves and relegated to the limbo of the nonpoetic. As I suggested earlier, the effect of such a theory is to sever the *process* or *act* of response from the intellectual *content* of the response, a procedure which divides sensibility and, in Mrs. Langer's case, results in a murky conflation of poetic meaning with music.

The psychologist C. G. Jung's theory that poetry springs from archetypes stored in a universal collective unconscious mind bears certain clear resemblances to the views of the philosophers of symbolic forms. Jung distinguishes between rational, objective, "directed thinking"—also termed "reality-thinking"—and the "fantasy-thinking" and dreaming of which poetry and myth are the objectification.[25] Jung's disciple,

---

23. *Feeling and Form*, p. 234.
24. *Ibid.*, p. 255. See also Northrop Frye: ". . . any poem with an idea in it is a secondary imitation of thought, and hence deals with representative or typical thought: that is, with forms of thought rather than specific propositions" (*Fables of Identity* [New York: Harcourt, Brace & World, 1963], p. 239.) and Susan Sontag: ". . . the knowledge we gain through art is an experience of the form or style of knowing something rather than a knowledge of something (like a fact or moral judgment) in itself" (*Against Interpretation* [Farrar, Straus & Giroux, 1966], p. 22).
25. *Symbols of Transformation*, I, 18.

Maud Bodkin, explores the parallels between psychological and dream processes and the techniques of poetry in her *Archetypal Patterns in Poetry*. She suggests, for instance, that the structure of tragedy is determined by the psychic pattern of ambivalence which arises out of a conflict between the personal, limited self and the aggressive fantasy-self.[26] This is the kind of primordial pattern which, according to Jung, "cannot be fathomed" by the conscious intellect; it can only be embodied in the complex images of poetry. The poet, Jung says, "must resort to an imagery . . . that is difficult to handle and full of contradictions in order to express the weird paradoxicality of his vision."[27] All of these doctrines have their parallel in Cassirer's phenomenology of the mythic consciousness.

Jung sharply distinguishes between the authentic and life-giving fantasies of the poet and creative artist and the infantile, autoerotic fantasies of the "autistic" mind characteristic of neurotics and schizophrenics.[28] Although such a distinction might be readily applied by a clinical psychologist working with living individuals or their case histories in front of him, this is not true of the literary critic, who is not at liberty to check his judgment against antecedent knowledge of his subject's behavior and condition. Since all fantasy-thought, like autistic thought, is inconsistent with a "rational and objective view of things,"[29] it is difficult to see how a critic might distinguish between authentic vision and mere pathological autism in a piece of writing.

This problem is intensified by the vagueness which surrounds Jung's doctrine of poetic truth. Jung says that "a great work of art is like a dream; for all its apparent obviousness it does not explain itself and is never unequivocal. A dream never says: 'You ought,' or: 'This is the truth.' It presents an image

26. *Archetypal Patterns in Poetry* (London: Oxford University Press, 1963), pp. 18–25.
27. *Modern Man in Search of a Soul*, trans. W. S. Dell and Cary F. Baynes (New York: Harcourt, Brace and Co., 1933), p. 190.
28. *Symbols of Transformation*, I, 28–29.
29. *Ibid.*, p. 29.

in much the same way as nature allows a plant to grow, and we must draw our own conclusions."[30] Such a position undermines the possibility of discrimination and judgment, and it is not surprising to find Jung admitting that the most psychologically interesting works are frequently those "of highly dubious merit."[31]

Northrop Frye and the Visionary Imagination

Cassirer and Jung's view of poetry as the objectification of primordial consciousness is echoed in the work of more recent myth critics, Northrop Frye being a case in point. Frye, though inspired chiefly by William Blake rather than by Cassirer or Jung, arrives at similar conclusions. Like them he begins with a distinction between man's "environment," the dead, unordered world of impersonal and indifferent nature, and man's "home," the human world which man creates out of his personal desires, a world with a "human shape and meaning."[32] Reason governs our transactions with the inert environmental world, giving us "a clear understanding of what is, as distinct from what we should like it to be." But reason "has no criteria for recognizing what is above itself"[33] and must therefore yield priority to imagination or "vision," which transforms the inert physical world into culture and civilization. "The world you want to live in is a human world, not an objective one."[34] Vision is totally autonomous, being the "pure uninhibited wish or desire to extend human power or perception (directly or by proxy in gods or angels) without regard to its possible realization."[35] The world of literature, which encompasses the totality of all works taken together, one vast

30. *Modern Man in Search of a Soul*, p. 198.
31. *Ibid.*, p. 177.
32. *Fables of Identity*, pp. 151–52.
33. *Ibid.*, p. 152.
34. *The Educated Imagination* (Bloomington: Indiana University Press, 1964), p. 19.
35. *Fables of Identity*, p. 153.

expression of "the total dream of man,"[36] is man's highest expression of vision, "a world completely absorbed and possessed by the human mind."[37] As in the mythical realm of metamorphosis and participation described by Cassirer, Frye's world of poetic vision permits no distinction between wish and fulfillment. Whereas reason shows us things as they are, "in the world of vision we see what we want to see."[38] In literature, as opposed to "assertive verbal structures," "the reality-principle is subordinate to the pleasure-principle."[39] "In the imagination anything goes that can be imagined."[40] "The creative process is an end in itself, not to be judged by its power to illustrate something else, however true or good."[41] Whereas reason gives us a nature indifferent to our desires, imagination and vision recapture "that original lost sense of identity with our surroundings, where there is nothing outside the mind of man . . ."[42] This sense of identity, however, should not be equated with belief or assent to objective truth, for poetry makes no statements about what is the case. "Poets think in metaphors and images, not in propositions,"[43] and in poetry "anything can be assumed. . . . there are no rights or wrongs and all arguments are equally good."[44]

What Frye does not appear to see is that his reliance on such terms as "desire" and "want" contains a fundamental confusion. "The world you want to live in is a human world, not an objective one," he says, ignoring the fact that most of us "want" to live in an objective world too, at least in the sense that we want our judgments and actions to be grounded upon something more than illusion and whim. If it is human to wish

36. *Anatomy of Criticism* (Princeton, N. J.: Princeton University Press, 1957), p. 110.
37. *Educated Imagination*, p. 33.
38. *Fearful Symmetry* (Boston: Beacon Press, 1962), p. 26.
39. *Anatomy of Criticism*, p. 75.
40. *Educated Imagination*, p. 29.
41. *Fables of Identity*, p. 148.
42. *Educated Imagination*, p. 29.
43. *Fables of Identity*, p. 33.
44. *Educated Imagination*, p. 77.

to flee the cold realm of objectivity, it is no less human to wish
to come to terms with it. We have a human "desire" to know
how things stand, regardless of whether such knowledge
makes us happy or not, and this desire cannot be arbitrarily
excluded from literature or consigned to the scientist or the
philosopher. The problem is *how* our desire for objective truth
enters into literature, how objective reality and the visionary
imagination are related—and here Frye can give no assistance
since he is unwilling to acknowledge that objective truth is a
consideration in literature at all. Just as Richards could discover no relation between the world of references and that of
emotive attitudes, so Frye can find no relation between the
objective world and the realm of myth, imagination, and "desire."

Frye's extreme position, however, is made somewhat easier
for him to maintain by virtue of his repudiation of value
judgments—or at least negative value judgments—as a respectable preoccupation of criticism. For Frye the ideal is "an
undiscriminating catholicity" of appreciation.[45] This rejection
of evaluations stems in part from Frye's wish to limit criticism
to scientific description and classification, but it serves the
further end of protecting Frye from the consequences of the
absence of any principle of critical discrimination in his theory
of imagination. Many commentators have expressed disapproval of Frye's reckless abandonment of evaluation (Wimsatt,
Brooks, and Murray Krieger have been among the most pene-
trating in their criticisms[46]). It should be noted, however, that
Frye is only being absolutely consistent in following to their
logical implications the principles of organicism and autonomy
to which so many contemporary critics—Wimsatt, Brooks,

45. *Anatomy of Criticism*, p. 25.
46. See Brooks and Wimsatt, *Literary Criticism: A Short History*
(New York: Random House, 1957), pp. 709-11; Wimsatt, *Hateful
Contraries* (Lexington: University of Kentucky Press, 1965), pp. 17-20;
and the essays by Wimsatt and Krieger in *Northrop Frye in Modern
Criticism*, Selected Papers from the English Institute, ed. Murray Krieger
(New York: Columbia University Press, 1966).

and Krieger among them—have committed themselves. The view that the imagination is a law unto itself is incompatible with any theory of the *proper* nature and function of poetry. Theoretical generalizations purporting to characterize an autonomous discipline are inherently superfluous and irrelevant. If poetry is truly autonomous, then Frye is right and critical discriminations are meaningless.

The difficulties of Frye's view become apparent in his major work of practical criticism, *Fearful Symmetry*. Because Frye adheres in the book to the principle of imaginative autonomy, Blake's own extreme subjectivism must be the standard against which Blake's poetry is measured. Consequently, this poetry is found not only to be uniformly great, but paradigmatic of the poetic mode of perception in its essence. Even though a great deal of the book is devoted to an exposition of Blake's intellectual position, the problems inherent in that position are never so much as mentioned. For example, Blake's contempt for the antinomian implications of Locke's epistemology is applauded by Frye, but no account is taken of what would appear to be an even more violent antinomianism in Blake's own outlook. ("Everything possible to be believed is an image of truth"; "reality is in the individual mental pattern."[47]) There is no reason why all criticism must be evaluative, and Frye's special purpose in his study was to elevate Blake's stature by refuting the uncritical stereotype of Blake as a mere eccentric or madman. But would not Frye have better accomplished this aim had he permitted the reader to feel that everything which issues from Blake's imagination is not validated by virtue of its having issued from Blake's imagination, that not quite *anything* goes that can be imagined? Since Blake has been tested against standards which cannot but vindicate him, the uncommitted reader is likely to feel that the critic, for all his aggressiveness, is too timid to risk exposing his subject to criticism.

47. *Fearful Symmetry*, pp. 19, 28.

Although Frye generally adheres to the principle of undiscriminating catholicity, he occasionally retreats from this principle and thus invites further difficulties. Frye is reluctant to see literature as purely "a wish-fulfillment dream."[48] Such genres as tragedy and satire, he says, present "a world . . . devoted to suffering or absurdity," and he holds that in the greatest literature we get both the tragic and the comic—"the up and down views, often at the same time as different aspects of the same event."[49] This is perhaps true, but it represents an implicit renunciation of Frye's carefully constructed position. For if we ask *why* the presentation of both "up and down views" should be thought a feature of the greatest works, the obvious answer is that such a presentation is ultimately truer to reality, more comprehensive in understanding, than the kind which recognizes the existence of only a single dimension. If we attempt to avoid this conclusion by saying that such literature is really only more *pleasurable,* we have still to account for the greater pleasure, and we are forced to the view that what is finally more pleasurable is what impresses us as most true. In other words, we betray our initial premises by implicitly subsuming the pleasure principle by the reality principle. A similar self-betrayal occurs when Frye, in discussing the morality of literature, says that literature presents vice and cruelty not to appeal to "any pleasure in these things" but to make us "see them for what they are,"[50] an odd notion to be coming from one who proclaims the imagination's liberation from "things as they are."

Thus, in spite of their tone of assurance, Frye's writings reflect evidence of the vacillation, ambivalence, and evasiveness which we have found to be characteristic of antipropositional theorists in general. Frye wishes to emancipate the imagination from all empirical and objective considerations, yet he also

48. *Educated Imagination,* p. 98.
49. *Ibid.,* p. 97.
50. *Educated Imagination,* p. 100.

77

aims at what he calls "the educated imagination," and he insists that literature "refines our sensibilities."[51] But the concept of "refinement" is meaningless apart from some sort of appeal to reality and the reality principle. Frye is forced, at critical points, to abandon the doctrine of autonomy which, most of the time, he is content to expound in the most extreme terms.[52]

Just as Jung had been unsuccessful in making applicable to literary criticism his distinction between the authentically visionary and the autistic, Frye attempts—and fails—to clarify a distinction between the "imaginative" and the merely "imaginary." If "in the imagination anything goes that can be imagined," then the infantile and the autistic must be received without complaint. As Murray Krieger points out, Frye "can urge but he cannot earn a distinction between 'the creative and the neurotic.' "[53]

Philip Wheelwright: Antipositivist Semantics

Philip Wheelwright's *The Burning Fountain* is one of the most comprehensive attempts to discuss poetry in terms of the mythic consciousness. Wheelwright compiles a list of the assumptions underlying the use of "literal language," also called

51. *Ibid.*

52. This is not the only contradiction to disturb the clarity of Frye's argument. In *The Educated Imagination* Frye adduces Stevens' poem "The Motive for Metaphor" in order to illustrate his point that poetry stems from "a desire to associate, and finally to identify, the human mind with what goes on outside it," and thus to achieve the "genuine joy" of unity. Frye finds in the poem the idea that poetry transforms the objective world, "the ABC of being," the "dominant X," into an imaginative world possessed and absorbed by the human mind (pp. 30–33). What is curious here is that Frye should be willing to take a poem as if it asserted a discursive proposition. A poem which says something about the relationship between poetry and objective reality can scarcely be said to be independent of objective reality. How can the poem corroborate Frye's argument without in the process destroying it?

It is worth noting that other critics have ascribed to this poem a more ambivalent attitude toward the imagination. J. Hillis Miller reads it as a categoric rejection of "metaphor and all its appurtenances" (*Poets of Reality* [Cambridge: Harvard University Press, 1965], p. 246).

53. *Northrop Frye in Modern Criticism*, p. 20, n. 10.

"steno-language." These assumptions are the "limiting conditions" which govern practical discourse. To mention a few of these limiting conditions, literal language is marked by distinctness between symbol and referent, univocation, and obedience to the law of contradiction. The conditions of "expressive language," on the other hand, are the reverse of these: iconic signification (i.e., identity of symbol and referent), "plurisignation," and obedience to the "principle of paradox," according to which "two statements which by the canons of strict logic are mutually contradictory, may sometimes be jointly acceptable."[54] Whereas steno-language conveys a bare report of empirical fact, expressive language, by virtue of what Wheelwright calls the "ontological status of radical metaphor," is "a medium of fuller, riper knowing" than is available through logical generalization,[55] and so on, through other antitheses familiar to the student of Cassirer and Jung.

M. H. Abrams, reviewing Wheelwright's book, argues that "by merely converting his refutation of the semantics of scientific language into the principles of his own poetic theory, . . . Wheelwright remains, in an important sense, a prisoner to the theory he opposes. For he . . . accepts as his own primitive proposition the typical positivistic opposition between scientific and expressive language. . . ."[56] Because Wheelwright's theory is controlled, in negative fashion, "by the alien requirements of a scientific logic and semantics," Abrams feels that it is "less than adequate to illuminate the nature and structure of poems."[57] Like many other anti-positivists, Wheelwright has unintentionally acceded to the positivism he opposes by removing poetry from the realm of rationally grounded knowledge and placing it in a transcendental realm. Furthermore, by defining poetry as positivism-turned-inside-out, as it were,

54. *The Burning Fountain* (Bloomington: Indiana University Press, 1954), pp. 52–75.
55. *Ibid.*, p. 97.
56. "The Newer Criticism: Prisoner of Logical Positivism?" *Kenyon Review*, XVII (Winter, 1955), 143.
57. *Ibid.*

Wheelwright permits "the alien requirements" of the positivist to dictate the terms on which—and in which—poetry is to be defined.

Wheelwright's conception of metaphor is crucial to his theory and typical of much recent thinking on the subject. Metaphor, by producing a fusion of two or more images, gives a "sudden perception of an objective relation" previously not noticed.[58] This fusion presupposes the "principle of paradox" by producing an identification of objects previously distinct and unconnected. Metaphor overrules the law of contradiction by saying that two different entities *are* one and the same. This principle of paradox resembles Cassirer's "law of metamorphosis," although Wheelwright's acknowledged source is the anthropologist Lévy-Bruhl's "law of participation." "Participation implies real identity, . . . a transcendence of either-or, an ontological overlapping by which emotionally congruent things, qualities and events blend into oneness."[59] This view of metaphor as involving a mysterious identification is one of the most frequently cited arguments for the theory that poetry transcends logic and statement. Frye, with characteristic bluntness, points the moral: "As for metaphor, where you're really saying 'this *is* that,' you're turning your back on logic and reason completely, because logically two things can never be the same and still remain two things."[60] Thus, metaphor is "inherently illogical."[61] Through metaphor, the poet emulates the primitive magician, who imputes *mana* to objects and deifies them, capturing that sense of lost rapport with nature

58. *Burning Fountain*, pp. 94–95.
59. *Ibid.*, p. 180.
60. *Educated Imagination*, p. 32. See also *Anatomy of Criticism:*
   In the anagogic aspect of meaning, the radical form of metaphor, "A is B," comes into its own. Here we are dealing with poetry in its totality, in which the formula "A is B" may be hypothetically applied to anything, for there is no metaphor, not even "black is white," which a reader has any right to quarrel with in advance. The literary universe, therefore, is a universe in which everything is potentially identical with everything else (p. 124).
61. *Fables of Identity*, p. 141.

which logic, reason, and the dualistic differentiation of consciousness have destroyed.

Morse Peckham has recently objected to the "unanalyzed equivalence of metaphor with poetry," a habit which frequently reflects a vested interest on the part of the theorist "in poetry of periods in which innovative metaphor, highly developed, is common."[62] But an even more serious ground for suspicion of this theory is its claim, sometimes concealed, sometimes overt as in Wheelwright, that metaphor carries with it certain ontological commitments. What Frye, Wheelwright, and others are saying is that the poet's use of metaphor inescapably commits him, provisionally at least, to a kind of transcendentalist monism. All truly poetic metaphor, as opposed to mere logical comparison of likeness or similarity, is held to imply a monistic identification of subject and object, general and particular, symbol and referent, mind and body, matter and spirit, and myriad other polarities, and thus to constitute a refutation of the rational, dualistic way of viewing the world. As Frye says:

> A world of total simile, where everything was like everything else, would be a world of total monotony; a world of total metaphor, where everything is identified as itself and with everything else, would be a world where subject and object, reality and mental organization of reality, are one. Such a world of total metaphor is the formal cause of poetry.[63]

Because the rational, dualistic world-view produces monotony, poetry, which respects the pleasure principle above the reality principle, prefers the consolations of monism. And because poetry is monistic, it cannot contain assertion or contradiction, it cannot *negate*. As Mrs. Langer says, "since presentational symbols have no negatives, there is no operation whereby their

---

62. *Man's Rage for Chaos: Biology, Behavior, and the Arts* (Philadelphia: Chilton Books, 1965), p. 127.
63. *Fables of Identity*, p. 249.

truth-value is reversed, no *contradiction*."[64] Or, in Kenneth Burke's formulation, "In imagery there is no negation, or disjunction. Logically, we can say, 'this *or* that,' 'this, *not* that.' In imagery we can but say 'this *and* that,' this *with* that,' 'this-that,' etc."[65] It thus appears that according to this theory a poet cannot possibly say in his poem that subject and object are *not* one, that matter is *not* spirit.[66] If he should go ahead and try to say this anyway, he cannot but fail, since his metaphors will automatically convert his would-be dualism into monism. Of course he may succeed in saying what he wants by eschewing metaphor, but then he ceases to be a poet, having betrayed his art by stooping to the use of steno-language and logic. Naturally, if he is a true poet, he will presumably have no interest in *saying* anything—he will seek to "embody" his meaning. But a theory according to which the poet is free to embody only a particular ontological view is surely a gratuitous and limiting theory.

What is more, it is clear that at this point the arguments of this group of mythopoeic critics come close to undermining the foundations of antipropositionalist theory. For if the poet's dependence upon metaphor implies a commitment to a particular ontological view, a special, visionary way of seeing the world, then objections to a propositional theory of poetry are weakened. Not only do poems now seem to assert propositions, but they seem always to assert the *same* propositions. "Literature," says William Troy, "is inclined toward one view of reality and science toward another."[67] This "one view of reality"—"*the* myth," as Troy sometimes calls it—embraces such doctrines as the inertness and meaninglessness of the

64. *Philosophy in a New Key*, p. 222.
65. *A Grammar of Motives* (New York: Prentice-Hall, 1945), p. 246, n. 3. See also Cassirer: "For myth there is no . . . not-being in which the being, the 'truth' of the phenomenon is grounded . . ." (*Philosophy of Symbolic Forms*, II, 63). See also Sigurt Burckhardt, *Shakespearean Meanings* (Princeton, N. J.: Princeton University Press, 1968), pp. 33-34.
66. See the discussion of "antivisionary poetry" below, pp. 118-25.
67. *Selected Essays*, ed. Stanley Edgar Hyman (New Brunswick, N.J.: Rutgers University Press, 1967), p. 33.

"objective" world, the alienation from nature and the self forced upon man by the modern, analytic mind, the desirability of a reintegration, by means of imaginative power, of subject and object, past and present, matter and spirit, power and justice, etc. I do not see why this "view of reality" should be exempted from classification as an abstract philosophy, a philosophy no less stable within a series or system of propositions than is Dante's Thomistic realism or Pope's Shaftesburian rationalism. The mythopoeic critic will assert, as Troy asserts, that the poetic vision is self-contained and "serves no extraneous ends,"[68] and that the poetic view of reality defies abstract formulation, but his words belie him at every step. To attribute to literature a capacity to express a view of reality is necessarily to concede that literature is not wholly self-contained and that it makes assertions.

Wheelwright departs from the main traditions of mythopoeic criticism in that the truth claims he makes for poetry are objective and more than psychological. He declares that "mythic utterances at their best really mean something, make a kind of objective reference, although neither the objectivity nor the method of referring is of the same kind as in the language of science."[69] He objects to Frye's "oversimplified distinction between outward and inward directions of meaning," ironically—in view of Frye's Blakeanism—terming it a "quasi-Cartesian dualism," and he challenges Frye's statement that "in all literary structures the final direction of meaning is inward."[70] Wheelwright asserts frankly that poetry gives "intuitions into the Beyond" and a knowledge of a "mysterious Other," a "primordial mystery."[71] He is thus willing to venture that poetry makes a kind of assertion. On the other hand, he

68. *Ibid.*, p. 205.
69. *Burning Fountain*, p. 4.
70. *Metaphor and Reality* (Bloomington: Indiana University Press, 1962), p. 180, n. 4.
71. *Burning Fountain*, p. 15; "Poetry, Myth and Reality," in *The Modern Critical Spectrum*, ed. Gerald J. and Nancy M. Goldberg (Englewood Cliffs, N. J.: Prentice-Hall, 1962), pp. 310–11.

distinguishes sharply between the propositional statements of steno-language and the "expressive" statements of poetry and myth, and here his seemingly straightforward advocacy of the truth claims of poetry is compromised by the same sort of equivocation we have found in other critics. The conclusion of the "Ode on a Grecian Urn," Wheelwright says, is a "truth in context," and he adds that we should be "willing to accept the partial truths of the insights which are crystallized by a given poetic mood without insisting that their truth must extend indefinitely into all other moods and contexts."[72] Coming from one who sees poetry as a higher form of knowledge, this is disappointing. It is a truism that no assertion, in poetry or elsewhere, is true in *all* contexts. What we want to know is whether the truth of a poetic assertion extends to *any* contexts outside the "mood and context" of the poem in which it occurs. By holding that the truth of Keats's statement is relative to its internal context, Wheelwright succumbs to a contextualist subterfuge and begs the question of poetic truth.

But even if his invocation of the truths of the Mysterious Beyond were not compromised by this kind of contextualist evasion, Wheelwright's vague metaphysics would not be a satisfactory basis for a poetics. Wheelwright goes farther than Frye by affirming a real metaphysical entity as a basis for poetic truth, not merely a "sense" of belief devoid of content. But his conception of what this content is is too ill-defined, as M. H. Abrams charges, to be of much usefulness. As Eliseo Vivas complains, Wheelwright fails to make good, or even make clear, his claims for the "ontological status of radical metaphor."[73]

The Circularity of Mythopoeic Theory

Thus the theories of the mythopoeic critics, like the theory we found in Richards, see poetry as an emotive use of language,

72. *Burning Fountain,* p. 301.
73. "A Semantics for Humanists," *Sewanee Review,* LXIII (Spring, 1955), 307–17.

84

independent of empirical canons of truth and falsity. Its purpose is to restore to the uncongenial and indifferent world of objective reality a subjective sense of identity, wholeness, and value. Accordingly, the aim of mythopoeic theorists, like that of Richards, must be to establish an internal or psychological sanction for poetry, so that poetry may become self-justifying in its independence of external reality. In each instance, the aim entails a severe divorce between rational discourse and poetry and hence a rigidly compartmentalized and dissociated conception of mental response.

Cassirer's and Jung's analyses of the processes of mythical thought are rewarding, and they have proved to be more fruitful for subsequent practical criticism than have Richards' hypotheses about neural impulses, disequilibriums, and harmonies. But it appears to me that in attempting to follow Cassirer's dictum that the "measure and the criterion" of the truth of mythical forms of thought must be found within "these forms themselves," the critics with whom we have been concerned in this chapter become involved in the same sort of circular and tautological reasoning which vitiated the theories of Richards. Just as Richards' psychological theory of value, by making emotive satisfactions an independent law unto themselves, was prevented from arriving at a principle of critical discrimination, so Frye's autonomous world of vision and Cassirer's, Wheelwright's, and Jung's world of primordial consciousness, in which everything participates in and merges with everything else, in which there is no distinction between what is and what we would like to be, and in which merely to be imagined is to be real, are likewise beyond the scope of criticism. In contrast to Richards, it is true, mythopoeic critics often make ambitious truth claims for poetry, but the truth to which they refer necessarily turns out to be vague, unverifiable, subjective, and finally indistinguishable from what Richards calls emotive belief. Like those of Richards, the theories discussed in this chapter are crippled by the absence of precisely the kind of critical principle which the initial axioms of these theories forbid as "extraneous."[74]

74. I am indebted in this chapter to an unpublished essay, "Northrop Frye and the Tradition of Archetypal Criticism," by my former colleague at Stanford University, William S. Marks.

CHAPTER FOUR

Cleanth Brooks:
New Critical Organicism

This chapter examines another kind of organic, antipropositional theory, one which defines the poem as an autonomous, self-contained entity—as a poem "and not another thing"—rather than as a means of producing emotive effects or a vehicle for the communication of archetypal content. New Critical theory, as we shall refer to it for convenience, locates the essence of the poem within the internal structure of the poem itself rather than in the nervous system of the reader or in the collective unconscious, and this theory claims as a consequence to have avoided many of the difficulties which attend the theories of the critics we have been examining. How well this theory actually succeeds in avoiding those difficulties we shall attempt to judge by examining closely the theory of a representative New Critical theorist, Cleanth Brooks.[1]

1. Treating Cleanth Brooks as representative of the New Critical view should require little defense. Brooks frequently acknowledges the closeness of his views to those held by Tate, Wimsatt, Blackmur, and Robert Penn Warren. John Crowe Ransom, although also often classified as a "New Critic," a term he helped to coin, departs from the mainstream of organic theory in significant ways and thus is not extensively discussed

Poetry and Ideas

We may enumerate several distinct senses in which, for Brooks, poetry is "dramatic" rather than propositional. (1) Poems communicate to the reader not directly but through the agency of a dramatic persona engaged in responding to a situation, whose speeches are arranged so as to be "in character" rather than objectively true. (2) Poetry is not organized according to the model of logical exposition but seeks to dramatize prelogical, associative states of consciousness. "I question," says Brooks, "whether the parts of any poem ever attain any tighter connections than the 'psychological' or that the coherence, even of the metaphysical poets, is not ultimately a coherence of attitude. To ask more than this, I believe, is to ask that poetry be something that it does not pretend to be: philosophy."[2] (3) "Any 'statement' made in the poem bears the pressure of the context and has its meaning modified by the context." Therefore, "poems never contain abstract statements."[3] Just as any single character in a drama interacts with other characters and the setting and is influenced

---

in this study. Ransom permits in a poem a "logical core" or "structure" of paraphrasable argument, upon which the poet builds an irrelevant "local texture," and this acknowledgment of the necessity of logic and statement, if only as a necessary evil, separates Ransom sharply from his colleagues and gives him a certain corrective force. See his extensive critique of Richards in *The New Criticism* (Norfolk, Conn.: New Directions, 1941) and his objections to Brooks's denial of logical organization in the same volume (See below, p. 108.). But Ransom's structure-texture distinction has been attacked by Brooks and others as a decoration theory, which, in my opinion, it is; for Ransom does not establish any functional connection between logical structure and irrelevant texture. On the other hand, Ransom shares with the other New Critics the conviction of the irrelevance of belief and truth to poetic value, the insistence on the importance of metaphor as a means of expressing a specially poetic way of looking at the world, and a suspicion of abstract, rational thinking.

2. *The Well Wrought Urn* (New York, Harcourt, Brace & Co., 1947), p. 221.

3. "Irony as a Principle of Structure," in *Literary Opinion in America*, rev. ed., ed. Morton Dawen Zabel (New York: Harper & Brothers, 1951), p. 731.

by them, so any statement in a lyric interacts with its verbal context and is modified accordingly. Philosophical generalizations must be read "as if they were speeches in a drama," expressing a partial viewpoint which is not to be identified with the assertion of the poem as a whole. The poem as a whole is a "little drama," whose structure of ironically counterpoised and conflicting attitudes resembles the conflict-filled structure of drama: "Most of us are less inclined to force the concept of 'statement' on drama than on a lyric poem; for the very nature of drama is that of something 'acted out'—something which arrives at its conclusion though conflict—something which builds conflict into its very being."[4]

If Brooks were merely arguing that poetry characteristically *implies* its meanings through the play of dramatic juxtapositions rather than relying on overt generalizations, it would not be difficult to follow his point. It might be objected that such a view is more applicable to a certain kind of poetry than to *all* poetry, but his theory would nevertheless be clear: poetry asserts ideas, but it does so through implication and indirection rather than explicitly. Although Brooks at times appears to be saying only this, he often goes much farther by suggesting that it is improper to talk of poetry as asserting or implying any statement whatsoever. The ambiguities in his theory become particularly evident in his treatment of the so-called "heresy of paraphrase." Of critical paraphrases in general, Brooks says:

> We may use—and in many connections must use—such formulations as more or less convenient ways of referring to parts of the poem. But such formulations are scaffoldings which we may properly for certain purposes throw about the building: we must not mistake them for the internal and essential structure of the building itself.[5]

The figure of the scaffolding, it may be interesting to note, seems to have been borrowed from Richards, who employs it

4. *Well Wrought Urn,* pp. 186–87.
5. *Ibid.,* p. 182.

in a similar manner in his discussion of *The Waste Land* in *Principles of Literary Criticism*. Richards there says that the separate "items" of the poem "are united by the accord, contrast, and interaction of their emotional effects, not by an intellectual scheme that analysis must work out." He adds that the reader may, if he so desires, make a "rationalization" of the experience by constructing an intellectual scheme, but that if he does so he will be "adding something which does not belong to the poem. Such a logical scheme is, at best, a scaffolding that vanishes when the poem is constructed."[6] Richards' use of the analogy raises a number of questions, for it is not apparent how *The Waste Land* can be fully appreciated apart from an understanding, in abstract terms, of its theme. Surely the proposition which Brooks finds there, "that men have lost the knowledge of good and evil" and that this "keeps them from being alive,"[7] has not been arbitrarily imposed on the poem. There seems to be a sense in which the proposition "belongs" to the poem, even though it is nowhere explicitly stated. If the idea does not belong to the poem, then what is its relation to it? One suspects that Richards' notion of an exclusively psychological coherence merely reflects his old difficulties over the relation of referential content to poetic response. And yet the coherence of psychological attitude which Richards finds in *The Waste Land* is precisely the kind of coherence which Brooks finds characteristic of *all* poetry and beyond which he thinks a poem ought never to go. On the other hand, Brooks's use of the figure of the scaffolding appears somewhat more moderate in its implications than Richards'. Whereas Richards, as regards one poem at least, sees the scaffolding as completely extraneous, Brooks appears to grant it a place in the poem, only cautioning that it should not be taken for the "internal structure" of the poem.[8] He is not always clear on this point,

6. *Principles of Literary Criticism* (Harcourt, Brace & World, 1928), p. 290.

7. *Modern Poetry and the Tradition* (Chapel Hill: University of North Carolina Press, 1939), p. 138.

8. Brooks appears to confuse the *semantic* (meaning) with the *syntac-*

however. Although he allows that we can formulate "propositions which seem to characterize, more or less clearly, the unifying attitude" of a poem, he warns that "to refer the structure of the poem to what is finally a paraphrase of the poem is to refer it to something outside the poem."[9] The phrase "outside the poem" leaves us in doubt as to what the paraphrase can be an "approximation" or "characterization" *of*. Are the ideas *in* the poem or not?

Brooks presumably means to say that the paraphrased ideas are *in* the poem in some sense, but that when we paraphrase them we reduce to a set of abstractions what are actually, in the poem itself, complex dramatic actions—experience embodied rather than ideas *about* experience. "A poem," he says, "does not *state* ideas but rather *tests* ideas. Or, to put the matter in other terms, a poem does not deal primarily with ideas and events but rather with the way in which a human being may come to terms with ideas and events."[10] In such formulations, Brooks seeks to credit poetry with an intellectual substance while averting the reductive implications of equating poetic meaning wholly with a set of stated ideas. But instead of solving the problem by seeing poetry as *both* a means of "testing" *and* "stating" ideas, Brooks indulges in the characteristic either/or of antipropositional theory, counterposing assertion and dramatization as irreconcilables. No one would deny that poetry "tests" ideas or that it deals with the way human beings "may come to terms with" ideas. But the rhetorical strategy in which "testing" and "coming to terms with" line up in opposition to "stating" and "generalizing" introduces a specious and unnecessary antithesis. Ideas, unlike physical substances, are not inert; to "test" an idea is to become committed

---

tic (structure) aspects of poetry here. It is one thing to hold that poetry has an unparaphrasable kind of meaning, another to hold that its structural connections are not logical. For a useful discussion of this distinction, see Murray Krieger, *The New Apologists for Poetry* (Minneapolis: University of Minnesota Press, 1956), p. 147.

9. *Well Wrought Urn*, p. 184.
10. *Well Wrought Urn*, p. 229.

to some intellectual point of view which emerges from the test. Of course, Brooks has in mind the dialectical qualification and ironic counterthrusts typical of the poetry he most admires, but he forgets that qualifications and revisions do not negate ideas but rather make them more subtle and complex.

Because he assigns "statement" to the nonpoetic pole of his antithesis, Brooks cannot finally make clear the connection between a critical paraphrase of a poem and the poem's meaning. In fact, it is unclear how there can be *any* connection if Brooks's assumptions are granted. The dramatic essence of the poem would seem to elude rational formulation entirely, so that no paraphrase could be anything but arbitrary and imposed.[11] One paraphrase would then be as good as any other. Such a consequence is a logical outcome of extreme organic theory, and it is reinforced by the Bergsonian notions about reason discussed in Chapter One:[12] if reason and experience are disjunct, rational formulations can have no claim on the vital, dynamic stuff of the poem; all formulation is arbitrary and criticism is reduced to impressionism.

I admit to uneasiness in making these criticisms, since Brooks is manifestly not an advocate of impressionism, and the view that one critical formulation is as good as any other would be repugnant to him. Often he appears to be objecting only to the schoolmarmish reduction of poetry to prettified prose statement, surely a legitimate objection. But there are tendencies in

11. See above, Chapter One, n. 37, on the futility of attempting to speak conceptually about entities which have been defined as conceptually unformulable. Allen Tate provides a statement of the dilemma in a comment on religious discourse:

It is irrational to defend religion with the weapon that invariably discredits it, and yet this is what seems to be happening. I am trying to discover the place that religion holds with logical, abstract instruments, which of course tend to put religion in some logical system or series, where it vanishes (*I'll Take My Stand*, by twelve Southerners [New York: Harper & Row, 1962], p. 163).

If the word "poetry" is substituted for "religion" in this statement, we have exactly the New Critical dilemma concerning paraphrase. The belief that rational language cannot encompass the nonrational discredits theory and criticism at a stroke.

12. See above, pp. 14–17.

his thinking which force him toward a position which he himself would regard as untenable. As in Richards, the uncertain and ambiguous status of the paraphrasable "scaffolding" is symptomatic of a deeper problem, an inability to determine the function of intellectual content in poetry. Brooks does not wish to banish ideas from poetry and on the contrary often speaks as if the problem of poetic meaning derives from the fact that poetry asserts *so many* ideas rather than none at all.[13] But having denied that poetry asserts anything, and having argued that the paraphrase takes us outside the poem, Brooks is left with no means of accounting for poetry's intellectual substance. It is as if the reader were left standing on a scaffolding with the building nowhere in sight.

This inability to account for the place of ideas in poetry seriously compromises Brooks's well-intentioned advocacy of the cognitive claims of poetry. Brooks and the New Critics are suspicious of emotivist doctrines like those of Richards and Cassirer, which reduce poetry to emotive stimulation or mere illusion and fantasy. Wimsatt condemns Richards' severance of emotions from their cognitive grounds,[14] and Brooks attacks Mrs. Langer's view that belief is irrelevant to appreciation. Mrs. Langer had said that Wordsworth's "Intimations Ode" expresses "essentially the experience of having so great an idea [as that of transcendental rememberance], the excitement of it, the awe, the tinge of holiness it bestows on childhood. . . ." Brooks comments: "The poem expresses what it feels like to have so great an idea. But what of greatness? If the idea seemed trivial to the reader, would that fact not make a real difference?"[15] The objection is well taken, but it is odd to find

13. See his remarks on "Corinna's Going a-Maying," *Well Wrought Urn*, pp. 68–70.

14. "The Affective Fallacy" (with Monroe C. Beardsley), *The Verbal Icon* (Lexington: University of Kentucky Press, 1954), pp. 22–27.

15. *Literary Criticism: A Short History* (New York: Random House, 1957), pp. 706–7. The quotation from Mrs. Langer comes from *Feeling and Form* (New York: Charles Scribner's Sons, 1953), p. 219. Brooks says elsewhere that he subscribes to a cognitive theory (*Well Wrought*

Brooks making it. He himself had earlier endorsed Eliot's statement that poetry does not advocate certain beliefs but tells us "what it feels like to hold certain beliefs."[16] And of course Brooks has always objected that the procedure of judging the "greatness" or "triviality" of a poem's ideas as such means going outside the poem, inviting the heresy of paraphrase, and raising the problem of belief. Evidently Brooks is reluctant to dismiss considerations of intellectual and cognitive belief, but his conviction of the fallacy of assuming a propositional content in poetry makes it difficult for him to justify claiming for himself the kind of cognitive theory which he recognizes to be a needed corrective to emotivism.

The Principle of Dramatic Propriety

The consequence of Brooks's denial that poetry makes assertions is that he is forced to seek an intrinsic or contextual criterion by which poetry can be judged, a criterion which will not force the critic to go "outside the poem." His most notable approach to such a criterion is represented in his "principle of dramatic propriety," according to which the statements made in a poem, "including those which appear to be philosophical generalizations—are to be read as if they were speeches in a drama. Their relevance, their propriety, their rhetorical force, even their meaning, cannot be divorced from the context in which they are embedded."[17] For example, we would not think of asking whether Edgar's statement in *King Lear*, "Ripeness is all," is true or false. The question would be whether it is appropriate to Edgar's character and to the play as a whole. Lyrics ought to be read in the same fashion.[18] Thus

---

Urn, p. 231), but he also insists that the poet is "a maker," not a "communicator" (p. 69).

16. "Implications of an Organic Theory of Poetry," in *Literature and Belief*, English Institute Essays, 1957, ed. M. H. Abrams (New York: Columbia University Press, 1958), p. 69.

17. *Literary Opinion in America*, p. 731.

18. *Well Wrought Urn*, pp. 141–42.

the apparently propositional conclusion of the "Ode on a Grecian Urn" must be read and judged as a speech "in character,"[19] not as a proposition asserted about beauty and truth in the external world. Brooks adds that the principle of dramatic propriety "is the only one legitimately to be invoked in any case."[20] By adopting this principle rather than one which holds the poem responsible for the empirical truth or falsity of its statements, we "insure our dealing with the problem of truth at the level on which it is really relevant to literature,"[21] for we have "waived the question of the scientific or philosophic truth of the lines."[22] Brooks adds that "if we can see that the assertions made in a poem are to be taken as part of an organic context, if we can resist the temptation to deal with them in isolation, then we may be willing to go on to deal with the world-view, or 'philosophy,' or 'truth' of the *poem as a whole* in terms of its dramatic wholeness."[23] It is not clear where this last argument leaves the principle of dramatic propriety. On the one hand, the principle is said to be "the only legitimate test"; on the other hand, we may, after duly applying the principle, "go on" to judge the world-view and truth of the poem as a whole. But when we go on to judge the world-view, are we not subordinating dramatic appropriateness to external correspondence and reintroducing questions of philosophic truth which we have just waived? Surely we ask more of someone's world-view than that it be "in character."

In short, Brooks vacillates over the question of coherence and correspondence, and in fact such vacillation reappears in all of Brooks's discussions of poetic criteria, poetic truth, and the problem of belief. On the one hand, Brooks disqualifies "abstract philosophical yardsticks," which encourage critics to go "outside the poem" to judge it. On the other hand, borrowing his terms from Eliot, Brooks says that a good poem is one

19. *Ibid.*, p. 151.
20. *Ibid.*, p. 142.
21. *Ibid.*, p. 152.
22. *Ibid.*, p. 142.
23. *Ibid.*, p. 152.

whose unity is "coherent," "mature," and "founded on the facts of experience,"[24] although he is careful to reject Eliot's implication that these qualities are to be sought in some implied propositional content. Brooks attempts to make Eliot's case "stronger still by frankly developing the principle of dramatic propriety suggested by his statement and by refraining from attempting to extract any proposition from the poem at all." This he proposes to achieve by regarding as acceptable "any poem whose unifying attitude is one which really achieves unity ('coherence'), but which unifies, not by ignoring but by taking into account the complexities and apparent contradictions of the situation concerned ('mature' and 'founded on the facts of experience')."[25] Brooks claims that he has followed the principle of dramatic propriety here and thus obviated any need to go outside the organization of the poem, but it is scarcely possible to take these claims seriously. Clearly, to the degree that one judges poetry according to whether it is mature and founded on the facts of experience one is judging it no longer merely as speech in a drama but as a kind of commentary, and the criteria of judgment cannot be called intrinsic. Brooks's refusal to recognize this fact frequently leads him to make baffling assertions like the following: "We do not ask a poet to bring his poem into line with our personal beliefs. What we do ask is that the poem dramatize the situation so accurately, so honestly, with such fidelity to the total situation that it is no longer a question of our beliefs, but of our participation in the poetic experience."[26] Once we introduce considerations of accuracy, honesty, and "fidelity to the total situation," we cannot very well maintain that our "personal beliefs" about what constitutes an accurate assessment are irrelevant. Nor does it help to try to evade the doctrinal implications of criteria like "maturity" and "accuracy" by converting these categories, as Brooks attempts to do, into

24. *Ibid.*, p. 228.
25. *Ibid.*
26. *Literary Opinion in America*, p. 740.

terms of inclusion and awareness of complexity. Admiration for inclusive awareness is itself an expression of a view of reality. As Morris Weitz shrewdly points out, "Brooks prefers the inclusive, the nonsimplification of attitudes, because he *believes* it to be a *truer* conception of human experience than the exclusive or sentimental simplification of attitudes."[27]

Much of Brooks's confusion appears to be a consequence of his gratuitous separation between "abstract philosophical yard-sticks" and "the facts of experience," a separation which, again, is traceable to the Bergsonian assumptions about abstract ideas discussed in Chapter One. What is a critic's sense of the facts of experience, after all, if it is not his "philosophy"? Brooks appears to think he can circumvent the need for abstract philosophical criteria by appealing to down-to-earth-sounding qualities like depth, maturity, and tough-mindedness, when, of course, he merely introduces his own preferred set of abstract yardsticks—and in a footnote appended to the discussion in question he concedes as much, in effect retracting his entire position.[28]

But here it might reasonably be objected that Brooks's difficulties stem primarily from excessive eagerness to relate the poem directly to the world of human values and knowledge, and that he would have strengthened his position had he remained faithful to his principle of dramatic propriety and his analogy between a poem and a speech in a drama. In other

27. *Philosophy of the Arts* (Cambridge: Harvard University Press, 1950), pp. 159–60. Weitz makes a number of significant points in objecting to Richards' and Brooks's theories. In reply to Richards' statement that "it is never what a poem *says* which matters, but what it *is*," Weitz says: "But this assumes that what a poem *is* is completely unrelated to what it *says*, and this is an unwarranted assumption since . . . part of what a poem is, is what it says, where 'says' is synonymous with 'statement' or 'truth claim' " (p. 159). In his chapter "Art, Language and Truth," Weitz sets forth and amply illustrates the thesis that art frequently asserts propositions and makes truth claims (pp. 134–52). See also Weitz's *Philosophy and Literature* (Detroit: Wayne State University Press, 1963).

28. *Well Wrought Urn*, pp. 228–29 n. Compare the similarly conciliatory footnote in *Principles of Literary Criticism*, pp. 272–73 n.

words, Brooks's vulnerability lies not, as I have been arguing, in his refusal to grant assertion to poetry but rather in his appeal to criteria like maturity, tough-mindedness, and the facts of experience, which covertly presuppose that poems *do* assert. If Brooks had rested his case on the contextualist or "structuralist" principle of dramatic propriety, he would have avoided the confusions and inconsistencies for which he has been taken to task here.[29]

Plausible though it sounds, this objection fails to take into account the peculiar difficulties presented by the principle of dramatic propriety. These difficulties arise because of the imperfect nature of the analogy between the lyric poem and the speech in a drama. In a short poem involving a single speaker the only means by which a reader may determine the nature of the context is by attending to what the speaker is willing to disclose to him. In a play the context is objectively established through the setting, the speeches and actions of various other characters, and the development of the plot, all of which are experienced by the audience independent of the speeches of any single character. The context of a short lyric, on the other hand, is necessarily filtered through the psychological state of the persona and is not separable from that state. There are, in other words, no external conventions, no independent setting or other characters, which can provide an index to the reliability of the viewpoint of the persona. There is thus an important sense in which the state of mind of the persona of a lyric *is itself* the "context" of any statement made in the poem. It follows that the request for contextual or dramatic appropriateness is circular unless supported by a demand that the persona be in some sense reliable in his account of his objective situation, that is, unless an appeal is made to something outside the self-enclosed "experience" of the poem itself. If no such

29. This is substantially the criticism leveled against Eliot's criteria of "maturity" and conformity to "the facts of experience" by Wellek and Warren (*Theory of Literature*, 3d ed. [Harcourt, Brace & World, 1962], p. 246), and leveled against Brooks himself by R. S. Crane. See my comments on Crane below, Chapter Five, pp. 125–27.

appeal can be made, then statements in a short poem cannot but be "in character" in that the state of mind of a persona must always be appropriate to itself. The speaker, for all we shall be able to tell, will always say just the sort of thing it is like him to say, and the poem will validate itself in every instance. If, for example, the speaker should speak confusedly, whatever it is in his "context" that confuses him must be communicated through the subjective medium of his confusion. Consequently, his confused utterances will invariably be appropriate to the poem's context—i.e., confusion. Similarly, even flagrant inconsistency or incoherence will be judged appropriate to an internal order whose contextual principle is inconsistency or incoherence. Again, experience becomes its own justification.

Despite the uncritical character of this viewpoint, it is widely held that the business of the poet is to present vividly and plausibly what it feels like to experience particular possibilities of experience and that the critic can legitimately demand no more of him than that. Whether the experience has any foundation in objective reality is irrelevant. Thus William Empson says with respect to poetic truths, "you are asked to imagine a state of mind in which they would *appear* true. True perhaps within a particular world of experience, maybe a narrow one, but true somewhere."[30] Northrop Frye says, "When we meet an unfamiliar experience in literature, the relevant question is not, is this true? but, is it imaginatively conceivable?"[31] Delmore Schwartz applies this principle to the poetry of Thomas Hardy, asserting that if the poet can get "the actuality of his experience into his poem," this is sufficient. "It does not matter whether that actuality is illusory or not; just as the earth may be seen as flat. The functioning of his sensibility guarantees his asserted beliefs; it guarantees them as

30. *The Structure of Complex Words* (London: Chatto and Windus, 1952), p. 12.
31. *The Well-Tempered Critic* (Bloomington: Indiana University Press, 1963), p. 149.

aspects of experience, though not as statements of truth."[32] In practice, this principle permits Brooks to excuse sentimental passages in the "Intimations Ode" on the ground that the speaker's "straining to work up a gaiety that isn't there" is "dramatically quite appropriate,"[33] or to R. P. Blackmur's declaration that Yeats's later poetry represents an "emotional possibility"[34]—really only a feeble compliment to the poetry. There is no telling what convulsions of self-pity and hysteria might not be justified as "imaginatively conceivable." All poems—good or bad—represent emotional possibilities; otherwise they could not have been written. The trouble is that almost any response might reasonably be held to be dramatically plausible, given a temperament or "sensibility" of a certain kind, and there is no way of obtaining information about this temperament aside from what is given in the words of the poem.

Here we arrive at the chief weakness of the "contextualist" or "structuralist" position, which sees the poem as a unique, self-validating cosmos, possessing its own independent "reality" apart from the external world. This view is advanced only equivocally by Brooks, whose contextualist affirmation of the self-validating nature of the poem conflicts with his allegiance to an ideal of experiential and moral truth. The doctrine of the total independence of the poetic "world" is more unqualifiedly

---

32. "Poetry and Belief in Thomas Hardy," in *Modern Literary Criticism*, ed. Irving Howe (New York: Grove Press, 1958), p. 350. Schwartz does not say how one decides whether the poet has gotten the actuality of his experience into the poem or not, or how one is supposed to test "actuality" without concerning oneself with truth. Interestingly, this doctrine would logically imply an elevation of *sincerity* and invite the charge of intentional fallacy.

33. *Well Wrought Urn*, pp. 124–25.

34. *Language as Gesture* (New York: Harcourt, Brace & Co., 1952), p. 83. See also Graham Hough's *An Essay on Criticism* (New York: W. W. Norton & Co., 1966):

When the reader's actual beliefs do not coincide with the poet's exhortations . . . the reader accepts the poet's statement as a possible point of view, one of the varieties of human experience, and makes an imaginative identification with it. He reads it as the dramatic utterance of a character whom he can understand (p. 80).

asserted by such critics as Eliseo Vivas, Wellek and Warren, and Earl Wasserman. Wasserman presents the case for the doctrine in particularly concise terms:

> Although [discursive] language is successive we can state simultaneity; we can describe a philosophy that denies the separateness of subject and object. That is, we can so arrange the preconceptions in our language that it asserts contrary conceptions. But it cannot, as discursive language, validate these conceptions by embodying them in the structure of the language. This validation, or affirmation, requires the formulation of the autonomous poetic reality in which the self-sufficiency of the poem is itself the validation. The concept is "true," or "real," because it is inherent in, rather than asserted by, its own self-containing poetic cosmos.[35]

To say that a poem "validates" conceptions merely by "embodying" them in an autonomous poetic reality is merely to equate the dramatic presentation of an idea with the justification of it. It is not specified according to what notion of "validity" the mere presentation of a viewpoint becomes a guarantee of its value. But if presentation *did* guarantee validity, what presentation would *not* be as valid as any other?

35. *The Subtler Language* (Baltimore: Johns Hopkins Press, 1959), p. 10. It should be noted that one critic who dissents from this view that there is a self-contained poetic world is I. A. Richards. He rejects the account of poetry

> . . . in terms of a supposed universe of discourse, a world of make-believe, of imagination, of recognized fictions common to the poet and his readers. A pseudo-statement which fits into this system of assumptions would be regarded as "poetically true"; one which does not, as "poetically false." This attempt to treat "poetic truth" on the model of general "coherence theories" is very natural for certain schools of logicians; but is inadequate, on the wrong lines from the outset. To mention two objections out of many; there is no means of discovering what the "universe of discourse is on any occasion, and the kind of coherence which must hold within it, supposing it to be discoverable, is not an affair of logical relations. . ." (*Science and Poetry* [New York: W. W. Norton & Co., 1926], pp. 68–69).

Of course, contemporary advocates of "coherence theories" of poetry would not hold that poetic truth or coherence is "an affair of logical relations." On the "sophism" of Croce's theory of "self-significance," see Edgar Wind, *Art and Anarchy* (New York: Vintage Books, 1969), p. 134.

Again, we are imprisoned in a circularity of reasoning according to which all "possible" or "conceivable" views are equally valid, so that the very notions of "validation" and "truth" become meaningless.

This is not to deny that there is a sense in which a poem, like any other piece of writing, may be said to "validate itself" by determining the standards against which it is to be judged. This sense depends upon our acceptance of generic classifications which exist outside the composition itself and which predetermine the reader's expectations. Thus, the book I am now writing may be said to determine the evaluative standards that should be applied to it: it would be unfair if it were judged as if it were a cookbook, a manual on railroading, or a novel. But it would be nonsensical to conclude from this that this book is an autonomous, self-referential organism, measurable only according to "laws of its own." All written compositions give indication, through their substance and form, of the preexisting generic categories under which they are subsumed and in terms of which they must be judged. Only in this sense does the concept of "self-validation" have any meaning.

Naturally, neither Brooks nor any of the other theorists who espouse a version of the principle of dramatic propriety or the theory of the autonomous context *intends* to surrender to the notion that anything goes in poetry or that any subjective experience is authenticated by virtue of its mere possibility. Innumerable statements in the work of these writers suggest that the poetic presentation must be rooted in an intelligent and humanly sound outlook, not merely a conceivable one. Unfortunately the prior commitment to the theory of the nonpropositional and autonomous nature of poetry inhibits these critics from developing the full implications of their reliance upon so openly external a criterion as intelligence or soundness. Clearly, once such criteria have been admitted, dramatic coherence has been subsumed by ethical and philosophical standards. This is not to reject the criterion of contextual consistency. I am only pointing out that this criterion alone is not sufficient.

The Language of Paradox

The concepts of "the language of paradox" and "irony as a principle of structure" are perhaps the best-known features of Brooks's poetic theory. A "paradox" is a verbal complex in which apparently conflicting ideas and feelings, whether stated explicitly or suggested through figurative nuances, are entertained simultaneously. "Irony" refers to the pressure of mutual modification and qualification which these ideas and feelings exert upon one another—the way in which each "undercuts" the force of the other. Both terms come into play in order to describe the structural pattern of successive "thrust and counter-thrust" and its resolution or synthesis. It is through the use of paradox and irony that poetry allegedly achieves its nonlogical, nonpropositional kind of meaning and unity. The doctrine owes an obvious debt to Richards' theory of balanced impulses, and versions of it appear in the theories of Tate, Wimsatt, Empson, Krieger, and Robert Penn Warren, among others. The doctrine reflects a moral predisposition to honest doubt and self-questioning, as in Robert Penn Warren's view that the true poet "earns" or "proves" his vision by submitting it to "the fires of irony"[36] and Wimsatt's that "the man speaking in the poem will move, toward whatever his goal is, honestly, with a sense of the obstructions and drags, the limitations, in a word, the wholeness of the experience."[37]

There is no reason to challenge the contention that paradox and irony, and the wholeness and honesty of outlook which they involve, are valuable constituents of at least a great deal of poetry. Brooks's revelations of the intricacies of dialectical

36. *Selected Essays* (New York: Random House, 1958), p. 29.
37. *Hateful Contraries* (Lexington: University of Kentucky Press, 1965), p. 46.

qualification in poems are often very convincing, and his analyses enhance the effect of the poems for the reader who returns to them. What is not convincing, however, is the conclusion that this sort of dialectical complexity is antithetical to logic. But of course "logic" is assumed to be incapable of dealing with complexity and conflict. As Allen Tate says, "in poetry the disparate elements are not combined in logic, which can join things only . . . under the law of contradiction; they are combined in poetry rather as experience, and experience has decided to ignore logic. Experience means conflict, our natures being what they are, and conflict means drama. Dramatic experience is not logical." [38] The law of contradiction holds that nothing can be both A and not-A at the same time. But in poetry, as in experience, according to Tate, things *are* both A and not-A at the same time. Most of the paradoxes which Brooks uncovers in *The Well Wrought Urn* turn out to be of that kind which appears to baffle the law of contradiction: Herrick sees love both as "harmlesse follie" and "thoroughly serious"; Wordsworth sees maturity as at once a loss and a gain and sees nature as both friendly and sinister; Pope sees Belinda as both goddess and "frivolous tease"; Donne was "thoroughly aware that a woman was a biological organism," but he could at the same time assert that she was "a goddess, nevertheless."

But do these paradoxes actually transcend the limits of logic? As Morris Raphael Cohen, the logician, says:

There is . . . nothing in logic or nature to prevent the existence of complexes in which contrary tendencies are conjoined. The law of contradiction is that nothing can be both *a* and *not-a in the same relation*. But physical entities or complexes of relations admit and often demand contrary determinations within them. Of any given individual it may

38. *The Man of Letters in the Modern World* (New York: Meridian Books, 1955), p. 335.

be true to say that he is both generous and not generous at the same time. The truth of both these statements becomes clear and determinate if we draw a distinction and say he is generous to his family and in public charities, but ungenerous to his employees and economic competitors. . . . The law of contradiction does not bar the presence of contrary determinations in the same entity, but only requires as a postulate the existence of a distinction of aspects or relations in which the contraries hold.[39]

Brooks's and Tate's argument that poetic paradoxes are non-logical fails to take into account the "distinction of aspects or relations" of which Cohen speaks. What is more, their argument is often belied by their own analyses of poems. For example, Brooks finds in "The Canonization" this implied argument: " 'Because our love is not mundane, we can give up the world'; 'Because our love is not merely lust, we can give up the other lusts, the lust for wealth and power'; . . . 'Because our love can outlast its consummation, we are a minor miracle, we are love's saints.' "[40] "Because" here flagrantly calls attention to the existence of logical relations between the elements of the poem: insofar as the love is merely lust, it is not divine; but also insofar as it is something more than lust, it is divine. Donne specifies the logical grounds upon which the claims of the lovers' spirituality rest. The contradiction, according to Brooks's own account, is only an apparent one.[41]

Again, consider Brooks's reading of the well-known stanza

---

39. *Preface to Logic* (New York: Meridian Books, 1956), p. 87.
40. *Well Wrought Urn*, pp. 15–16.
41. Brooks obscures the issue when he says that poetic paradoxes are only "apparently" contradictions. Thus: The fusion which the creative imagination effects "is not logical; it *apparently* violates science and common sense" (*Well Wrought Urn*, p. 17 [italics added]). Does this mean that the paradoxes *really* violate science and common sense or that they only appear to do so? Again: the critic should regard as acceptable any poem which unifies "not by ignoring, but by taking into account the complexities and *apparent* contradictions of the situation concerned" (*Well Wrought Urn*, p. 228 [italics added]).

from Wordsworth's "She Dwelt Among the Untrodden Ways":

> A violet by a mossy stone
> Half hidden from the eye!
> Fair as a star, when only one
> Is shining in the sky.

Brooks notes the disagreement between the first two lines and the last two as evidence that the poem is "not organized logically." "Wordsworth has simply set down the comparisons side by side, with not an 'and' or a 'but' or a 'therefore' or a 'nevertheless' to relate one to the other. Are they related? Or do they cancel each other out? For if Lucy's loveliness is indeed scarcely visible, half hidden from the eye, how can she be as prominent as the evening star?"[42] In pointing to the device of "direct confrontation and juxtaposition" used by Wordsworth, Brooks is making a very useful observation about a certain kind of poetic procedure. But when he goes on to contend that the poem's structure can only be understood as an instance of what Laura Riding and Robert Graves call a "supra-logical harmony," he overstates his case, as his own further explanation of the poem makes clear. Brooks says: "Though Lucy, to the great world, is as obscure as the violet, to her lover she is as fair as Venus, the first star of evening. It is this contrast between her utter inconsequence to the world and her overwhelming importance to him that constitutes the theme that runs through the three stanzas."[43] That is, in one respect Lucy is inconsequential, in another, important. Again, once the implicit logical connections between images are discovered, their unity turns out not to be supralogical at all.

But, of course, it is possible to call into question Brooks's readings of these poems and to challenge his unwittingly logical explications of their paradoxes. Murray Krieger, although

---

42. "A Retrospective Introduction," *Modern Poetry and the Tradition* (New York: Oxford University Press, 1965), p. xv.
43. *Ibid.*, pp. xv–xvi.

he does not mention Brooks by name, appears to allude to him in the following remarks on "The Canonization": "To say, as a recent critic has said, that the poem celebrates the glories of a love that has more to it than lust, is seriously to cheapen and misrepresent it."[44] Krieger argues that the paradox of the poem is that the lovers in their earthiness must be accepted, in "defiance of our dull world of logic," "literally and not just figuratively as saints (totally *as* saints and not just in part like and in part unlike them) . . ."[45] That is, the lovers are both saintly and lustful, fleshly and spiritual, at the same time and "in the same relation," to use Cohen's terms once more. Krieger perceives very well that an analysis such as Brooks's unintentionally confirms the logical character of the poem.

There is something to be said for Krieger's reading of "The Canonization": the poem may indeed mean that flesh and spirit are one in a way that *is* a logical contradiction, a way that cannot be understood in terms of mere likeness or similarity of properties. Whatever the case with Donne, no one could seriously maintain that there are no poems in which logical contradictions do appear. But to acknowledge the occurrence of such contradictions in poetry is not to concur with the New Critics that it is the essence of all poetry to present nonlogical resolutions of conflicts. Many apparent contradictions in poems turn out, upon examination, to be capable of logical resolution according to the conventions set forth by Cohen in the passage quoted above. But when real contradictions occur in a poem, nothing requires us to posit some supraconceptual mode of understanding which perceives identities without respect to logical relations. For one thing, a contradictory meaning is one which can be apprehended in conceptual, propositional terms. In fact our recognition of contradictions *as* contradictions and our decision to overlook the contradictions we have recognized are dependent upon our acceptance of a logical frame-

44. *New Apologists for Poetry*, p. 18.
45. *A Window to Criticism* (Princeton, N. J.: Princeton University Press, pp. 7–8.

work. The poetic vision which appears to defy "our dull world of logic" by asserting the oneness of opposites depends upon existing logical conventions to give its defiance significance.

In a sense, then, there is no such thing as a "resolution" which is apprehended outside the context of logical relationships. As John Crowe Ransom argues in a critique of Brooks: "Opposites can never be said to be resolved or reconciled merely because they have been got into the same poem, or got into the same complex of affective experience to create there a kind of 'tension.' . . . if there is a resolution at all it must be a logical resolution . . . when there is no resolution we have a poem without a structural unity."[46]

Conclusion

The theories examined in the last three chapters are linked by their preoccupation with a concept of poetic autonomy: for Richards, autonomy is located in the neurological impulses of the individual reader; for the mythopoeic critic, it resides in the collective unconscious of mankind; for the New Critical theorists, autonomy is ascribed to the verbal context of the poem itself. It is the poem's context and meaning, not the emotions of the reader or writer, which are regarded as self-supporting and independent of discursive reason and empirical truth. But "the poem itself" has proved difficult, perhaps impossible, to talk about except in terms borrowed from some preexistent, extrinsic frame of reference. Despite their celebrated opposition to the imposition of alien categories upon the analysis of poetry, the New Critics themselves tend to rely upon a borrowed, extrapoetic framework as a basis for their own definitions of poetry and contextual autonomy, a fact which is evident when we note how thoroughly their critical vocabulary is pervaded by psychologically-weighted terms.

46. *New Criticism*, p. 95. The logical basis of poetic structure is argued more fully in Chapter Five.

Announced intentions notwithstanding, the New Critics, even in theory, treat poetry not "as poetry and not another thing" but rather as presentation of "experience," of states of mind. This concern with states of mind, to be sure, focuses upon objective properties within the poem's structure and not upon some ideal reader's nervous system or some racial consciousness. And like Jung and Cassirer, these critics emphasize the *objectifying* character of the poetic process, the way in which poetic form transforms the raw, personal emotions and opinions of the poet into an impersonal aesthetic construction. Nevertheless, the poem as the New Critics see it cannot be conceived as a purely aesthetic object; it is deeply implicated in human psychological processes, in psychic conflicts and resolutions. New Critical "contextualism" expresses many of the same theoretical impulses contained in Richards' theory of emotive autonomy and falls victim to many of the same difficulties.

As Murray Krieger has pointed out, there is in New Critical theories a "dedication to the existential," a respect for the mimetic and referential functions of poetry, which distinguishes these critics from Frye and other mythopoeic critics.[47] Nevertheless, Frye's theory of the autonomy of the imagination is only an extension of a principle shared with New Critical theory—the organic, nonassertive character of poetry. It is true that the New Critics press the claims of objectivity, truth, and maturity, but they fail to make clear how these things actually enter into the poem and how they can be validated. Similarly with their disagreements with Richards: if, as they frequently object, Richards fails to establish a connection between poetry and the objective world, the judgment must apply to them as well. T. S. Eliot, for example, very acutely objects that Richards wants "to preserve emotions without the beliefs with which their history has been involved." But the force of Eliot's criticism is dissipated when,

47. *The Play and Place of Criticism* (Baltimore: Johns Hopkins Press, 1967), p. 227.

one page later, he says that "the material of the artist is not his beliefs as *held*, but his beliefs as *felt*."[48] This, as far as I can see, is exactly what Richards was saying. Likewise, when Allen Tate says that in poetry "we get knowledge of a whole object," he appears to be departing radically from Richards. But when he says that this knowledge is "not knowledge 'about' something else; the poem is the fullness of that knowledge,"[49] it is fair to ask in what respect Tate has improved upon Richards. Since the New Critics cannot, without self-betrayal, establish a sense in which poetic truth is more than subjective and psychological, their theories can finally amount to little more than a restatement of Richards' doctrine of emotive truth or "Truth[E]"—the emotively gratifying feeling that All is One, ungrounded in anything save the feeling itself.

Their rejection of statement, logic, and the criterion of external correspondence forces the New Critical theorists to appeal to the subjective state of mind of the poem itself as if it somehow contained an inherent self-validating principle, whereas principles of validation must ultimately derive their sanction from outside the poem. The opposition of poetic and propositional meaning forces these critics to dissociate "experience" from its rational grounds and thus to assume with Richards that "experience is its own justification." The relativism and irrationalism which follow from this position are, of course, the last things these critics set out to endorse, and they rescue themselves, in a fashion, by a self-contradictory insistence upon external criteria like "maturity." Despite the strong absolutist impulse of many of these theorists, the pull of organicist theory is inevitably toward the subjectivism of Richards' psychological theory of value and hence the destruction of all objective standards. To transfer the concept of autonomy from the psychological realm of Richards to the contextual realm of Brooks is merely to relocate the problem of circular-

48. *The Use of Poetry and the Use of Criticism* (London: Faber and Faber, 1933), pp. 135–36.
49. *Man of Letters in the Modern World*, p. 63.

ity within a new frame of reference. New Critical "contextualism" is essentially Ricardian psychologism in new trappings; the theory is no more able to overcome the problem of subjectivism when set forth with a contextual and formalistic emphasis.

CHAPTER FIVE

Action and Argument

I n the last chapter, we discussed the widely held view that a poem should not have a logical structure. If the poem is to dramatize the tensions and conflicts of experience, it must be organized "psychologically," eschewing mediating abstractions and exposition. It is further held that the "pressure of the context" undercuts and qualifies all generalized affirmations and commitments. It is one of the legitimate achievements of the New Criticism to have shown how poems double back upon themselves, enriching and deepening their meanings through intricate networks of contextual cross-connection. But these very worthwhile adumbrations of the dramatic and complex nature of poetry are too frequently vitiated by over-simple and hasty conclusions. First, it is too readily assumed that *all* true poems are psychological rather than logical in structure. One need merely adduce a lyric by Greville, Nashe, or Jonson to refute this exaggerated contention. Second, it is misleading to speak of psychological structure, even where it is properly identified, as if it were wholly independent of logical determination. Even the most associative of lyrics usually possesses an implicit logical subject. Finally, it is too easily supposed that in a good poem the "pressure of the context" is always exerted in a single direction—that of ironic qualification and deflation. It is possible to produce many poems in which this pressure does not "undercut" but supports and reinforces a dominant thesis asserted by the poem.

On the other hand, it cannot be denied that for many poems the concepts of a psychological organization, of a "structure of resolved stresses," and of an ironically self-qualifying kind of meaning are relevant and applicable. If we compare two well-known poems by George Herbert, the differences between the alternative principles of organizational structure and meaning should become apparent.

Two Kinds of Poetry

"The Collar,"[1] the more "dramatic" of the two poems, presents a speaker whose words proceed fitfully from thought to thought, suggesting the spontaneous and unpremeditated processes of a mood of spiritual restlessness and rebellion:[2]

> I Struck the board, and cry'd, No more.
> I will abroad.
> What? shall I ever sigh and pine?
> My lines and life are free; free as the rode,
> Loose as the winde, as large as store.
> Shall I be still in suit?
> Have I no harvest but a thorn
> To let me bloud, and not restore
> What I have lost with cordiall fruit?

---

1. *Works*, ed. F. E. Hutchinson (Oxford: Clarendon Press, 1941), pp. 153–54.

2. This structural pattern is described as "qualitative progression" by Kenneth Burke, *Counter-Statement*, 2d ed. (Los Altos, Calif.: Hermes Publications, 1953), pp. 124–25. See also the discussion by Yvor Winters, *In Defense of Reason* (Denver: Alan Swallow, 1947), pp. 55 ff.

But the poem is dramatic in a further sense which involves contextual self-qualification. "I will abroad," for example, is counterbalanced by the implied suggestion that there is nowhere to go—that the presence of God is inescapable. The abrupt reversal at the end of the poem brings the conflict between rebellion and acceptance to a resolution:

> Away; take heed:
> I will abroad.
>
> . . . . . .
>
> But as I rav'd and grew more fierce and wilde
> At every word,
> Me thoughts I heard one calling, *Child!*
> And I reply'd, *My Lord.*

The poem resolves itself on the side of Christian acceptance and humility, but the feeling of acceptance is qualified by the earlier parts of the poem in which the claims of rebellion receive at least something of their due, so that neither "I will abroad" nor "My Lord" mean quite what they appear to mean when each is read apart from the other. The poem's structure reflects the "successive fireworks of contradiction, and a mind jumping like a flea" which William Empson discovers in another of Herbert's poems.[3]

"Church-monuments," in contrast, is undramatic in the senses of the term under consideration here. Its progression is not that of spontaneous processes, and it contains little in the way of ironic counterpressure. The poem is explicitly logical, expository, and propositional.

> While that my soul repairs to her devotion,
> Here I intombe my flesh, that it betimes
> May take acquaintance of this heap of dust;
> To which the blast of deaths incessant motion,
> Fed with the exhalation of our crimes,
> Drives all at last. Therefore I gladly trust

3. *Seven Types of Ambiguity* (New York: Meridian Books, 1955), p. 256.

My bodie to this school, that it may learn
To spell his elements, and finde his birth
Written in dustie heraldrie and lines;
Which dissolution sure doth best discern,
Comparing dust with dust, and earth with earth.
These laugh at Jeat and Marble put for signes,

To sever the good fellowship of dust,
And spoil the meeting. What shall point out them,
When they shall bow, and kneel, and fall down flat
To kisse those heaps, which now they have in trust?
Dear flesh, while I do pray, learn here thy stemme
And true descent; that when thou shalt grow fat,

And wanton in thy cravings, thou mayst know,
That flesh is but the glasse, which holds the dust
That measures all our time; which also shall
Be crumbled into dust. Mark here below
How tame these ashes are, how free from lust,—
That thou mayst fit thy self against thy fall.[4]

The method is figurative, but the various figures—of scholar-ship, heraldry, conviviality, etc.—are subordinated to the argu-ment. The body is mortal; "therefore," it must study its fate so that it may overcome its lusts and prepare for death. Much of the exposition is given in the framework of a lesson which the speaker addresses to his flesh. He entrusts his body to the "school" of the crumbling gravestones and monuments to learn of its impending dissolution in the "dustie heraldrie" of their inscriptions. Because there is a particularized setting, as in "The Collar," and because the speaker addresses us only indi-rectly, we may wish to say that the poem dramatizes the giving of the lesson—it presents a person in the act of "coming to terms" with the fact of mortality. We would go too far, however, if we concluded that because the poem is a dramati-zation of a man arguing, it therefore cannot be said to advance an argument. To take this approach is to distort the character

4. Herbert, *Works*, pp. 64–65.

of the poem and to obscure the difference between its structure and method and that of "The Collar." The lines

> That flesh is but the glasse, which holds the dust
> That measures all our time; which also shall
> Be crumbled into dust. . . .

assert a proposition which asks to be accepted seriously by the reader as a comment on experience. The fact that the proposition issues out of a dramatic framework does not limit its liability as a universal generalization.[5]

The pressure exerted upon these lines by the total context of the poem works in a reinforcing, not an ironic, direction. It is not that there are no subtleties in the argument or no sense of conflict; it is merely that nothing in the poem contradicts or ironically undercuts anything else. Herbert is not indulging in

---

5. This issue is raised in a controversy inspired by J. V. Cunningham's essay, "Logic and Lyric," *Modern Philology*, LI (August, 1953), 33–41 (reprinted in Cunningham's *Tradition and Poetic Structure* [Denver: Alan Swallow, 1960], pp. 40–58). Cunningham attacks the conventional view that "poetry and logic have nothing to do with one another" and adduces three poems whose structure is shown to be rigorously syllogistic: Marvell's "To His Coy Mistress," Dunbar's "Lament for the Makaris," and Nashe's "Adieu, farewell earth's bliss." Frank Towne replies to Cunningham's essay in "Logic, Lyric, and Drama," *Modern Philology*, LI (May, 1954), 265–68. Towne concedes that "in a certain sense" a poem like "To His Coy Mistress" may be said to be "logical in form," but since the poem is "a presentation of a situation" and since it is axiomatic that the logic in a poem "is always in a subordinate position, subserving the expression of emotion," such a poem cannot "in any sense be called logical." "The disinterested reader is simply presented with a situation—a presentation that has no relation to logic except in so far as logic is made use of by one of the characters." The inference is that anyone who regards a poem as logical cannot be a "disinterested reader." Towne declares that "any lyric is dramatic. Like other forms of art, it is presentational rather than discursive." "Logic [a poem] may contain, but the reader is not persuaded by that logic; or, if he is, such persuasion is quite incidental to the main activity in which he is engaged. It is not his business to be persuaded by it, or to reject it, but to note its operation in a total situation as it proceeds from the mind of a speaker." Again, we encounter the gratuitous assumption that the logical aspects of poetry are merely "made use of" for purely emotive ends and have no importance themselves; again, dogmatic assertions about "the main activity" of poetry and "the business" of poets and readers, as if these dictums do not even need to be argued.

ironic qualification when, after telling his flesh that it is doomed to crumble, he instructs it to prepare itself. The idea that the flesh should prepare for its fall is not introduced as a denial of the fact of that fall—there is no logical inconsistency. Flesh must learn of its fall "that"—in order that—it may prepare. "You are going to fall; therefore, ready yourself." The effect produced by the final line is thus to exert a reinforcing and supporting pressure on what has gone before, not to deflate it ironically. The statement of the inevitability of bodily dissolution means what it says.

Although "Church-monuments" is undramatic in its logical structure and contextually self-reinforcing meaning, there is yet an important sense in which the poem is dramatic. For all poems are dramatizations of states of mind, and this is true regardless of whether the poem is organized psychologically and associatively or by syllogism. "Church-monuments" dramatizes an attitude of brooding melancholy and sardonic, almost wry resignation. The poem makes a statement about the inevitability of death and dissolution and acts out a set of attitudes which are grounded in this statement and which serve to enrich it and give it depth and poignancy as felt experience. Despite its logical, expository character, the poem is as much a presentation of the *act* or *process* of thinking and feeling as is "The Collar."

Conversely, if there is a sense in which "Church-monuments" is dramatic, there is likewise a sense in which the organization even of a poem like "The Collar" must be acknowledged to owe something to logic. Despite the associative and spontaneous character of its development, certainly much closer to the structure of immediate consciousness than to that of logical thought, it can be seen that the poet nevertheless adheres to certain canons of logical relevance in his selection of material. The poem does not really approximate the flux of immediate consciousness but makes a selection within the limits of logical relevance determined by the subject. The poem's progression from thought to thought is not "determined" by logic in the sense that successive propositions follow consecutively from the last; the progression is ordered with regard to psychological probability—how a person of volatile temperament would be likely to react under the strain of a strict religious discipline. But the various aspects of the reaction are codetermined by the broad limits of logical relevance. There is nothing in the poem that is not relevant to the subject of spiritual rebellion. However erratic, hyperemotional, "fierce and wild" the ejaculations become, they do not digress from relevance to the logical subject on which the poem is grounded. Furthermore, even though no explicit propositions occur in the poem, the poem does *imply* an assertion, and this assertion plays an organizing role. The poem implies that however attractive rebellion may be, it is both dangerous and futile to run from God. Or rather, it implies that both rebellion and acceptance have their claims, and even though acceptance and humility are the wiser course, the course dictated by God's will, it is not always possible to adopt it. I am aware of the risk of reducing a complex poem to a mere platitude, but this danger does not alter the fact that an implied general comment does inform the poem and influences its construction.

Antivisionary Poetry

The kind of poetry represented by "Church-monuments," in which logical, expository structure is pronounced, tends to be relegated to second-class status by contemporary criticism—stigmatized as decorative poetry or put at a distance with the condescending label "poetry of statement." Even when such poetry is appreciated, it is seldom on its own terms. The view that logic is incompatible with experience has obscured the distinction between subtle, dignified generality of statement and crude, didactic preachment. However, the issue is one which transcends questions of poetic method. As we have seen, despite the antipropositional emphasis of contemporary theories, many of these theories rely on or presuppose a kind of metaphysical monism, and this monism easily becomes a doctrinal obligation. Poetry is supposed to present a world of transcendent identities, in which there occurs a coalescence of subject and object, symbol and referent, mind and body, historicity and timelessness, etc. The trouble is that there is a substantial body of poetry which does not express this monistic world-view, a poetry which defines its attitude in conscious opposition to this world-view, often rejecting it as sentimental consolation and illusion. In this antivisionary type of poetry, subject and object are *not* one; the subject is set over against an alien and inexpressive cosmos which provides no setting for sympathetic identification. Such poetry derives its emotion from the pathos of a world void of mythological and spiritual comfort; its conflicts and "tensions" are not subsumed by some overriding attitude of reconciliation. It achieves its resolutions by driving home the theme of the irreconcilability of conflicts. Such poetry is characteristically blunt and assertive in its tone, and when it employs metaphors at all it pays a good deal of attention to their illustrative functions. Often the imagery of the visionary tradition is employed, but with an ironic significance. Stevens' "The Course of a Particular," which was discussed earlier, is a poem of this antivisionary type. Another is Edwin Arlington Robinson's "Hillcrest."[6]

"Hillcrest" presents a speaker who is isolated as if on an island from the roaring of a world of conflict, change, and disorder, which he has temporarily left behind but to which he will have to return:

> No sound of any storm that shakes
> Old island walls with older seas
> Comes here where now September makes
> An island in a sea of trees.
>
> Between the sunlight and the shade
> A man may learn till he forgets

6. *Collected Poems* (New York: Macmillan Co., 1937), pp. 15–17.

> The roaring of a world remade,
> And all his ruins and regrets;

He stands between sunlight and shade, symbolically in neutral
territory between the sunlit world of pain and bitter knowledge and the shadowy realm of death and the blindness of
error. It is the familiar situation of the visionary poem: the
protagonist momentarily apart from the "din of towns and
cities" and apparently about to embark upon a private escape
into some more satisfactory world of imagination through
which he may "forget" change and the "ruins and regrets" that
it has worked upon him in the past. But here the stance is
self-consciously antivisionary; instead of turning to "more elevated thoughts" of pantheistic communion or to the allurements of "easeful death" and the obliteration of human distinctions, the speaker considers, in the ensuing stanzas, another
alternative:

> If, eager to confuse too soon,
> What he has known with what may be,
> He reads a planet out of tune
> For cause of his jarred harmony,—

> If here he venture to unroll
> His index of adagios,
> And he be given to console
> Humanity with what he knows,—

> He may by contemplation learn
> A little more than what he knew,
> And even see great oaks return
> To acorns out of which they grew.

The speaker turns back to a consideration of the facts of
experience in the world from which he has retreated and
attempts by careful discrimination and distinction to come to
an understanding of those facts. He attempts to master the
facts of change and unpredictability by reasoning about them
in as precise a manner as possible—and is not content simply to
present his state of mind in its desperation or to dramatize

various possibilities of approach. The first two stanzas above deal with an unsatisfactory alternative in terms of a logical proposition: if, remembering one's past misfortunes, one interprets the future glibly in terms of them—pretentiously rehearsing one's moralistic clichés ("adagios") for the supposed edification of humanity—one will have falsified reality by sentimentally imposing one's personal "jarred harmony" upon it. By attempting disinterested contemplation, one may finally be undeceived and thereby purged of this vanity. One may then come to understand the true causes of things, the "acorns" out of which one's fate grew.

> He may, if he but listen well,
> Through twilight and the silence here,
> Be told what there are none may tell
> To vanity's impatient ear;
>
> And he may never dare again
> Say what awaits him, or be sure
> What sunlit labyrinth of pain
> He may not enter and endure.
>
> Who knows to-day from yesterday
> May learn to count no thing too strange:
> Love builds of what time takes away,
> Till Death itself is less than Change.

Through contemplation one transcends the vanity of preconceptions and realizes that one can never presume to predict the course of things. One can never suppose confidently that the past is a sure index to the future or understanding a guarantee of happiness or the avoidance of pain. For whoever knows the present from the past knows that nothing is "too strange" in a world of mutability. To wit: love increases as time and change remove the objects of its attachment, until finally extinction itself appears less monstrous a prospect than continuing change. After this assertion of the conditions of true understanding, the poem concludes with a reconsideration of further wrong alternatives:

Who sees unchastened here the soul
Triumphant has no other sight
Than has a child who sees the whole
World radiant with his own delight.

Far journeys and hard wandering
Await him in whose crude surmise
Peace, like a mask, hides everything
That is and has been from his eyes;

And all his wisdom is unfound,
Or like a web that error weaves
On airy looms that have a sound
No louder now than falling leaves.

These stanzas repudiate visionary romantic idealism, which refuses to distinguish the emotions of the subject from the object. The vanity of seeing the world as radiant with the delight of the perceiver, the characteristic illusion of the child, is the inverse counterpart of the vanity described earlier of seeing the world in terms of one's disillusioned "jarred harmony," the tendency of the veteran cynic. Both involve a subjective and sentimentally imposed falsification in the interests of self-flattery. The poem states the consequences of this error, the aimless and empty sterility that will be the lot of him whose "crude surmise" blinds him to the truth. All his "wisdom" has no substance; it fades into silent invisibility before the fact of change. The final image, strikingly beautiful as it is, is yet rigorously grounded in the argument.

I have dwelt in detail upon this poem in order to suggest the subtlety and complexity achievable by the method of logical exposition when employed by a serious poet. The poem attempts to define by precise logical discrimination the extent to which knowledge is possible in human affairs. The poem is skeptical, but its skepticism is not total; understanding is limited but possible. The poem rejects not the possibility of knowledge but the possibility of certainty, and it specially condemns glib forms of certainty. We can never be certain of the accuracy of our predictions. We "may," by laborious application, come to understand the causes of past events, but we are vain if we take the past to be an infallible key to the future. As Brooks would point out, the poem is based on a paradox. But whereas Brooks's paradoxes are held to be the antithesis of logical argument, it is only in terms of logical distinctions that the paradox of knowledge in "Hillcrest" has any meaning: *in one respect* we can know reality; *in another respect* we cannot know it. Through such distinctions, complexities are acknowledged and dealt with, not excluded and ignored. If our vanity's impatient ear is unwilling to recognize the logical character of the poem, we will be deaf to its meaning.

It would have been possible for Robinson to employ a more dramatic method—to represent his speaker, say, as gripped temporarily by the successive vanities, finally to arrive at some conclusion through a process of thrust and counterthrust of conflicting commitments. But Robinson chooses to reason about the unsatisfactory alternatives rather than dramatically indulge in them. This does not mean that the speaker is not tempted by the allurements of a self-congratulatory cynicism or a childish idealism, for these are presented as possessing their satisfactions, but he rejects them nevertheless, and without vacillation. Similarly, where Robinson might have presented a dramatic exhibition of uncertainty, he writes about the inevitability of uncertainty in an authoritative manner. The poem gives no hard-and-fast "answers," as the method of logical exposition allegedly must do; the only answer put forth is that there are no easy answers. But in rejecting easy answers, the poem is blunt and unequivocal, bearing the reader down with an assurance and an imperturbability that has nothing to do with self-righteousness or glib solutions. The poem takes the risk of asserting something, exposing itself to criticism by the unapologetic candor of its posture. Not only in its abstract argument, but in its lucid expository form and its sullen, unequivocal feeling of stubborn rationality, Robinson's poem constitutes a poetic criticism of a whole literary tradition.

At this point, I imagine my reader thinking: this is all well and good, but what has any of this to do with poetry? Robinson may have composed some perspicuous generalizations, but that does not constitute a poem. Without a full employment of metaphor and imagery, the poet's vision cannot have been properly *earned*. But metaphor and sensory imagery, although often present in the greatest poetry, represent only one method of "earning" a poetic vision. Unadorned generalizations are not necessarily unpoetic; they are capable of being authenticated by a skillful handling of diction, rhythm, and movement. In the best passages of "Hillcrest," there is a tone of voice which lends to the poem's statements a sense of personal authenticity, a sense of issuing from a real human being immersed in the perplexities of circumstance. Consider the most abstract and general of the stanzas of the poem:

> Who knows to-day from yesterday
> May learn to count no thing too strange:
> Love builds of what time takes away,
> Till Death itself is less than Change.

These lines scan regularly without metrical substitutions, but in the second and third lines it is possible to detect a slight but significant variation in the length or quantity of the syllables. The last four syllables of line two and three of the last four syllables of line three are long. Three of these long syllables stand out noticeably because they occur in unaccented positions ("no," "too," and "time"). The sudden collocation of long syllables, occurring nowhere else in the poem, produces a distinct emotional heightening and gives a peculiar emphasis to what is being said at this point. This systematic use of rhythmic variation in order to convey the subtlest nuances of emphasis and perception—a unique characteristic of poetry—is an instance of what I have been attempting to demonstrate in this book: how a dramatic quality, an enactment of psychological attitudes through the implications of formal properties, enters even into the poetry of abstract expository statement in a functionally unified way. The rhythmic movement here permits the poem to "act out" a set of feelings grounded in the abstract propositions stated by the poem.

Logical Structure

My argument to this point conveys the implication that there are two radically opposed classes of poems—the logical, contextually self-reinforcing type and the psychological, contextually self-qualifying, "dramatic" type. Such a scheme would correspond to a recognized historical distinction between "traditional" and modern poetic methods. Few would wish to deny that an understanding of the conception of poetry as dramatic action, as a discourse in which psychic flux is more prominent than logical exposition, is indispensable for an appreciation of the poetry of Yeats, Pound, Eliot, Stevens, and other moderns. At the same time, in regard to medieval, Renaissance, and eighteenth-century poetry, it is obvious that modern critical categories are often inappropriate and need to be replaced, or at least corrected, by a recovery of the categories of traditional poetics. A sharp distinction between kinds of poetry, then, is a critical necessity. Yet such a distinction has its dangers: it may encourage us to overlook common principles in the aims and methods of poets of various periods and to accede too readily to an easy historical relativism according to which poetry becomes whatever the presumed spirit of the age happens to make of it.

These and other considerations, to my mind, vitiate the otherwise helpful distinction between "didactic" and "mimetic" lyrics advanced by R. S. Crane and Elder Olson of the Chicago group of critics. According to this distinction, didactic lyrics are those in which "the formal principles are clearly ideas."[7] Their structure involves some "pistic or argumentative

7. *The Languages of Criticism and the Structure of Poetry* (Toronto: University of Toronto Press, 1953), p. 190.

element."[8] Mimetic lyrics, about which these critics tend to be less clear, imitate actions of characters in particular situations. Whereas didactic lyrics seek to persuade, "to inculcate certain moral attitudes," mimetic lyrics aim to "give us a specific pleasure by arousing and allaying our emotions" and they make use of "our moral attitudes to arouse our emotions."[9] "Mimetic poetry," Olson says, "is not statement; doctrine appears, not as something urged, but as something assumed, and chiefly as what the poet assumes to be necessary or probable, or to be evocative of this or that emotion or moral attitude."[10]

But these distinctions raise more questions than they answer. It is not clear how one goes about determining whether in a given instance the doctrine is "something urged" or "something assumed." Does "The Course of a Particular" seek to "inculcate" the idea that "being part is an exertion that declines," or does it merely "make use" of the idea in order to arouse our emotions? To recall Erich Heller's observation, quoted earlier, one cannot "use" thought without thinking in the process. There must surely exist a substantial class of poems to which such clear-cut categorization does not apply, poems in which we find a mixture of didactic and mimetic aims and methods. Secondly, the Chicago critics' antithesis between didactic and mimetic lyrics leads them to a conception of the mimetic lyric which is remarkably similar to the view of poetry to which Richards and Brooks are led by their science-poetry antithesis. Olson, for instance, says that "poetic statements must not be confused . . . with propositions; since they are not statements about things which exist outside the poem, it would be meaningless to evaluate them as true or false."[11] That is a statement which might easily have been made by Richards or by any New Critic. In his critique of William

8. *Critics and Criticism: Ancient and Modern*, ed. R. S. Crane (Chicago: University of Chicago Press, 1952), p. 66.
9. *Ibid.*, p. 67.
10. *Ibid.*, p. 68.
11. "'Sailing to Byzantium': Prolegomena to a Poetics of the Lyric," *University Review*, VII (Spring, 1942), 216.

Empson's theory, Olson complains that the New Critics have ignored the distinction between "*lexis* and *praxis;* between speech as meaningful and speech as action."[12] But it is not clear that this distinction between language as *lexis* and as *praxis* differs significantly from the statement-drama distinction which is all-pervasive in the theorists whom Olson attacks. Similarly, Crane accuses Brooks of misrepresenting Gray's *Elegy* as "an emotionalized argument in verse," "not a poem but a piece of moderately subtle dialectic."[13] The poem ought rather to be read as "an imitative lyric . . . in which the speaker is conceived as being merely moved in a certain way by his situation."[14] In effect, Crane is urging upon Brooks Brooks's own principle of dramatic propriety, the circular nature of which has already been shown. Crane has good reason for objecting that Brooks has violated this principle, but he seems insufficiently aware that in terms of theoretical commitment to the principle itself he and Brooks are not far apart.

In short, although the distinction must always be kept in mind, there are dangers in too severe a polarization of lyrics of argument and lyrics of action. Even the lyric of action is seldom devoid of argumentative and logical elements, just as the argumentative poem is to an extent a dramatization. Harold H. Watts, in *Ezra Pound and the Cantos,* speaks to this point when he observes that, in spite of Pound's theories of the

12. *Critics and Criticism,* p. 54.
13. *Languages of Criticism,* p. 176.
14. *Ibid.* Crane praises Brooks's statements that philosophical generalizations in poems "are to be read as if they were speeches in a drama" and that a poem is an imitation by virtue of its "*being* an experience rather than any mere statement about experience . . ." (*Critics and Criticism,* pp. 94, 107). Crane's chief quarrel is that Brooks fails to adhere to these principles. Oddly enough, however, Brooks does appear to have satisfied Crane's requirements in his treatment of Gray's *Elegy:*

It ought to be . . . clear that the epitaph is not to be judged in isolation. It is part of a context. . . . We have to read it in terms of the conditions for a certain dramatic propriety which the context sets up. Among those conditions are these: it must be a recognizable epitaph, even a humble epitaph, modest in what it says, and modest, perhaps, even as an example of art. For it is the epitaph, after all, of a "Youth to Fortune and to Fame unknown" (*The Well Wrought Urn* [Harcourt, Brace & Co., 1947], p. 111).

ideogram and of "ideas in action," the end product of these theories "is not different in kind from the end-products of poets who handle language in a way that does not confuse us at all."[15] What Pound actually does in *The Cantos*, says Watts, "is different from what he judges he is doing." Language in its semantic aspect is ineradicably conceptual and abstract, and in attempting to subvert these aspects of language Pound "strives against the structure of man's mind itself." *The Cantos* actually have much to say, in general terms, about civilization, society, and the evils of usury, and the poem "urges on us participation in political and social action." "Ironically, the trouble with the ideas that organize the poem, that are served by the method of the ideogram, is that they are too general; they tend to make the tension of the poem as much a matter of black-and-white opposition as that of heaven to hell-mouth in medieval drama."[16] Watts's point here should serve to check the common tendency to overstate the claims of that poetry which allegedly goes in fear of abstractions. The presence of logical organization and conceptual meaning ought not to be ignored simply because the predominant tendency of a poem is subjective and associative, or because the notion of a special poetic "logic of the emotions," in Eliot's phrase, is sanctified by an impressive body of theory. In fact, it might be argued that the modernist attempt to achieve greater concreteness by cutting away the conceptual connections between images only dooms the poet to an even more abstract level of generality than that of traditional verse. The traditional poem, because it spells out its argument explicitly, does not so readily invite the sort of windy philosophical interpretation which readers and critics find themselves forced into when they attempt to make coherent sense of *The Waste Land* or *Paterson*.

Keats's "Ode to a Nightingale" is a prime example of the "poetry of experience," a poem in which there is no easily

15. *Ezra Pound and the Cantos* (London: Routledge and Kegan Paul, 1951), p. 121.
16. *Ibid.*, pp. 118–24.

identified core of general assertion. The "Ode" is a dramatization of the dynamic processes of the mind; its speaker exemplifies Keats's principle of negative capability by acting out various points of view, never settling upon any single attitude as a conclusive position. The poem's moods move by successive states: from drugged lethargy and dejection at the beginning, to an agonized longing for a saving vitality and creativity, to an abrupt and ecstatic identification with the nightingale and its unconscious happiness, to a longing for the total oblivion and selflessness of death, then back to a sense of the speaker's separateness from the bird, and finally to something resembling his original forlorn state. What is more, there are modulations and intermediate stages within each shift of mood, and all of the positions and stages are complicated by the conflicting tensions suggested by the poem's imagery. For example, the imagery of sleeping and waking, of drowsy, leaden eyes and beautiful, lustrous eyes, of visions and waking dreams, interpenetrates all the stages in various ways. The speaker "awakens" from his initial drowsiness by entering the dreamworld of the nightingale, where sleeping is in a sense a more wide-awake condition than the apparent wakefulness of everyday life. But he still longs for a further, even more authentic, sleep of death, and at the end of the poem he is uncertain whether he is awake or asleep. Sleeping and waking are thus played against each other in a series of metaphoric transformations pregnant with meanings.

But we would be mistaken if we concluded from all this that the poem eschews reason and logic. Everything in the poem, despite the incessant shifting of positions, is relevant to a central problem—stated in its broadest terms, the problem of the epistemological status of imaginative perception. The issue raised is that of whether the imagination, identified with the singing of the nightingale and associated with human dreaming and artistic creation, represents a truer mode of apprehension of reality than everyday rational perception. Everyday perception apprehends a kind of reality, but it is an inert and unsatisfying kind which is terrifying in its revelations of change, decay, and suffering and which leaves the perceiver sick and enervated. He may "forget" this kind of reality by entering the imaginative dreamworld of the nightingale, in which he can apprehend an entirely different reality, more mysterious and ill-defined, but far more satisfying. Man's capacity for realizing this dreamworld, however, is severely limited, since the organic realm of nature always exceeds him in its perfection. Furthermore, the more creative, pleasurable, and vital world of imagination, when pursued to the limits of man's capacity, leads to disintegration and death. If the sleep of imagination is the most desirable state, this sleep can only be attained at the expense of a total surrender and annihilation of the self. As Earl Wasserman has pointed out, the speaker is suspended between "two conflicting sets of standards": the ideal of vigorous sensation and ecstasy conflicts with the ideal of personal self-preservation.[17] The problem, then, may be seen as one of mediating between the contradictory claims of sleeping and waking. We seem to be in touch with reality when awake in the everyday world, but perhaps the imaginative world glimpsed through poetry and dreams is truly more real. The sleep of poetry appears to redeem us from the death of waking mortality, but only to propel us toward another death —the surrender of our identity. Which of the two realms is finally more real? Which, finally, should one choose to pursue? The speaker is able to give no decisive answer to these questions, hence his uncertainty at the end of the poem. As in "Hillcrest" (although Keats's style and sensibility are entirely different from Robinson's), the poem raises questions about the nature of knowledge and concludes that these questions cannot be answered conclusively; there are antinomies and contradictions at the heart of experience. This ultimate proposition about the indeterminacy of experience is a governing presupposition that conditions the movement of the poem,

17. *The Finer Tone* (Baltimore: Johns Hopkins Press, 1953), p. 183.

which is fluid, shifting, hesitant, and tentative. As in "The Collar," the sequence is not determined by logic in the sense that each successive thought is deducible from the last; on the contrary, the poem advances from stage to stage in a way which suggests the spontaneous processes of reflection as they take shape out of whimsical and associative lines of connection. Still, there are rationally explicable threads of conceptualization interlacing every element of the poem and within whose limits of relevance everything in the poem remains.

Given the logical character of even so dynamic and apparently alogical a poem as Keats's "Ode," what can we conclude concerning our previous distinction between poems of psychological and logical organization? The first thing to be said is that such a distinction is misleading if it is taken to mean that there are, on the one hand, logical poems, and on the other, poems wholly devoid of logic. We would do better to redraw the distinction as one between expositorily patterned poems, in which logical organization is overt and explicit and is reflected in a consecutive ordering of elements, and poems in which there is no overt logical exposition, but in which a logical subject and a general conceptualization are implicit in the dramatic unfolding of an action whose primary determinant is a mirroring of prelogical processes. In the one kind of poem, logic is more plainly the determinative structural principle of the poem and emerges as overt, consecutive argument. In the other kind, logic serves to limit and condition the framework of subject matter and relevance within which the associative and psychological processes are dramatized.

Antipropositional theorists tend to assume that wherever generalizations and arguments appear openly in a poem, they must have been "imposed" or "forced" upon it from "outside." This view, it seems to me, reflects a confusion over the concepts of "inside" and "outside" and a misconception about the way in which abstract interpretations and judgments enter into a piece of writing. It is assumed by organic theory that the interpretive and judgmental aspects of a poem can be somehow inherent in the mere action itself, as if the presentation of raw experience could contain its own interpretation of itself apart from the mediation of a conceptual framework. However, when an interpretation appears to arise naturally out of the dramatic stuff of action, without explicit or overt commentary, the interpretation has nevertheless been put there—infused into the language, the tone, the selection and ordering of the details of the action—by a conceptualizing intelligence, and if the action is coherent, its coherence is referable to a conceptual scheme. The conceptual scheme, the interpretation, in such a case, is neither more nor less "imposed" from "outside" than if it had been asserted in a series of propositional statements accompanying the action. Whether or not an interpretation is "imposed" and inorganic has nothing to do with whether it is asserted explicitly or is allowed to be implied through the action. An "imposed" or "forced" interpretation is merely one which is irrelevant to the context of experience that is established as the focus of the poem, one which does not follow from what is said in the rest of the poem or which our experience tells us is a false or arbitrary conclusion concerning the kind of subject matter dealt with by the poem. The didactic conclusions of some of Longfellow's lyrics are illegitimately "imposed"—not because the conclusions are explicitly asserted but because they are not logically implied by what has gone before and violate our sense of what conclusions properly apply to the kind of experience Longfellow is writing about.

A poem of explicit propositional argument like "Hillcrest" cannot, then, be judged, prima facie, less "organic" than a poem of dramatic enactment like the "Ode to a Nightingale" purely on the basis of the poetic method employed. Abstract interpretations are as much present in Keats's poem as in Robinson's, and these interpretations are "inside," not "outside" the poem, even when they must be indirectly inferred.[18]

18. In *The Poetry of Experience* (New York: W. W. Norton & Co., 1963), Robert Langbaum's discussion of these issues runs sharply counter

Admittedly, poetry of the kind which indulges in overt statements has its own generic limitations: a tendency toward
overassertiveness, a danger of lapsing into frigid rhetoric and
platitude, a hollowness that is felt when the propositions are
not informed by the energy of conviction and discovery. But
such poetry also possesses virtues which the kind of poetry
that eschews general statements is likely to lack: an engaging
willingness to put matters in the bluntest terms, an honest
vulnerability which is not afraid to risk exposure, a refusal to
take refuge in a coyly protective self-qualification or a safe,
diplomatic identification with all sides of a question.

To put the argument of this chapter in the plainest terms,
the poem whose elements are not connected by some logical
thread, some relevance to a logical subject, is to that extent an
incoherent poem. There are, of course, other means of achiev-
ing unified effects in poetry: unity of rhythmic structure, of
tone, of imagistic texture, etc. But unity of structure is preemi-
nently a logical matter, for without a unity of subject, these

---

to the present account. Langbaum locates "the essential idea of romanticism" in "the doctrine of experience—the doctrine that the imaginative
apprehension gained through immediate experience is primary and certain, whereas the analytic reflection that follows is secondary and problematical" (p. 35). Thus the poetry of the nineteenth and twentieth
centuries is "a poetry which makes its statement not as an idea but as an
experience from which one or more ideas can be abstracted as problematical rationalizations" (pp. 35–36). In contrasting the "primary" claims
of immediate experience with the merely "problematical" categories of
"analytic reflection," Langbaum sums up the theoretical position which
has been criticized throughout this book. Langbaum's account of the
theoretical basis of the "poetry of experience" is illuminating, but it fails
to take into account the weakness of the theory's chief assumptions, or,
rather, it regards this weakness as an unavoidable legacy of modernism.
The "doctrine of experience" assumes uncritically that language has
access to a primary level of consciousness and is capable of freeing itself
from the abstract and the categorical. The consequence of a doctrine
which sees conceptual meanings as mere "rationalizations"—ideas which
may be abstracted from the poem but are not really contained in it—is a
wholesale critical impressionism. If a poem can mean whatever any of its
"problematical" interpretations attribute to it, then poetic meaning has
become indeterminate and interpretation is arbitrary. This is precisely
the difficulty encountered by Brooks in his treatment of the heresy of
paraphrase (see above, Chapter Four, pp. 89–94).

other kinds of unity will seem incomplete. There is no logic of the imagination, no purely psychological coherence outside a mediating framework of logic. Without a logical subject, there is nothing around which attitudes can cohere.[19] As Henry David Aiken has observed,

> when we ascribe "coherence" or "unity" to a work of art . . . we are merely giving evidence of the artist's power to evoke and sustain an integrated system of beliefs. The sensory and imaginal content of a work of art does not establish its own unity as an aesthetic whole; nor do its parts "fit" together simply because they coexist. What is required if the elements are to be composed into an aesthetic whole is the presence of an ordering system of beliefs and attitudes which make them mutually relevant to one another.[20]

In other words, the imaginative "fusion" or synthesis of disparate experiences, which is often thought to be the peculiar organizing principle of poetry, involves no transcendence or supersession of logic. I share the skepticism of Radcliffe Squires, who argues that "the esemplastic imagination, alas, never existed—there is no faculty charged with the duty of fusing detail into a single meaning or effect. Fusion takes place in a poem, as in other forms, because of syntax within language; or because of a guiding concept which may be openly postulated or allegorized by a symbolism."[21] Whatever impli-

19. See above, Chapter Four, p. 30.
20. "The Aesthetic Relevance of Belief," in *Aesthetic Inquiry*, ed. Monroe Beardsley and Herbert Schueller (Belmont, Calif.: Dickinson Publishing Co., 1967), p. 145.
21. "Mr. Tate: Whose Wreath Should Be a Moral," *Aspects of Modern Poetry*, ed. Richard M. Ludwig (Columbus: Ohio State University Press, 1962), pp. 271–72.
The theory of alogical fusion has been most recently restated in an essay by George Lensing and Ronald Moran, "The Emotive Imagination: A New Departure in American Poetry," *Southern Review*, N. S., III (Winter, 1967), 51–67. The "emotive imagination," the authors maintain, leads the reader to understanding through feeling and "irrational leaps" rather than through "chartered and structured intellectuality." A passage from William Stafford's poem, "Fall Wind," is adduced

cations this statement may have concerning the process of creation in the poet's mind, a subject outside the scope of this inquiry, Squires is justified in calling into question the organicist claims of alogical, "esemplastic" fusion in the poetic product. Even Coleridge, we ought not to forget, held that the synthesizing imagination is "retained" under the "irremissive, though gentle and unnoticed control," of the will and understanding.[22]

A final test case presents itself in the conclusion of T. S. Eliot's *Four Quartets*, a poem whose form and content is deeply saturated in the traditions of antirationalist poetics:

> Quick now, here, now, always—
> A condition of complete simplicity
> (Costing not less than everything)
> And all shall be well and
> All manner of thing shall be well
> When the tongues of flame are in-folded
> Into the crowned knot of fire
> And the fire and the rose are one.[23]

The fusion of disparates culminates in the last three lines, where, by metaphoric transference, the fire is spoken of in

---

as an example of this kind of poem (in *Traveling through the Dark* [New York: Harper & Row, 1962], p. 70):

> Pods of summer crowd around the door;
> I take them in the autumn of my hands.
>
> Last night I heard the first cold wind outside;
> The wind blew soft, and yet I shiver twice:
>
> Once for thin walls, once for the sound of time.

The authors say that the "leap" at the end of the poem is "structured emotionally, not rationally." But is this really the case? The poem seems to be about growing old. The first two lines establish a contrast between the summer of the natural setting and the autumn of the observer, a clear anticipation of the idea of age and the passage of time stated in the final line. I see no irrational leap at all. Moreover, the idea of an "emotive imagination" seems to me neither new nor a departure.

22. *Complete Works*, ed. W. T. G. Shedd (New York: Harper & Brothers, 1853), III, 347.

23. *The Complete Poems and Plays, 1909–1950* (New York: Harcourt, Brace & Co., 1950), p. 145.

terms of the rose and the rose in terms appropriate to the fire. "Tongues of flame," an apocalyptic image which carries an additional suggestion of devourment, are said to be "infolded," as if they were rose petals, into a "crowned knot," an image which suggests intertwining and unity, royalty and traditional order, as well as floral arrangement. What fuses these diverse associations is not some nonlogical, esemplastic unity, but the familiar principle of relevance to what Aiken calls "an ordering system of beliefs and attitudes." Each of the disparate implications and suggestions is logically related to the overriding argument of the *Four Quartets:* the interdependence of suffering and redemption, the identity of the longing and pain of man's limited, temporal life with the beatitude of the still point out of time and space. Once the reader has taken possession of this guiding concept, the images take on their full and proper significance and the emotional intensity of the lines becomes explicable and reasonable. The fire-rose cluster of images, in short, is bound together by the crowned knot of logical relevance, and it requires no invocation of a mysterious imaginative fusion to explain the unity. Outside the context of Eliot's argument, of course, no necessary connection exists between fires, roses, tongues, and crowns. It is Eliot's argument which makes these objects relevant to one another by subsuming them under an overriding conceptual framework.[24]

24. The priority of conceptualization spoken of here pertains to relations within the poem, not necessarily within the mind of the poet before or during the process of composition. It should not be supposed that the theory advanced here necessarily involves a mechanistic or rationalistic psychology of the creative process. When I speak of the organizing influence of conceptual argument and logic, of the controlling intelligence which infuses its interpretations throughout the action of the poem, I am not offering a hypothesis about the temporal sequence which takes place in the poet's mind. A good deal of misleading theorizing has been derived from the legitimate insight that poets normally *discover* their meaning only through the process of writing the poem. The fact that a poem is usually the end product of a process of exploration and discovery, rather than predetermined in advance, in no way implies that the poem cannot have a logical or expository form. Expository prose writers frequently find that what they really want to say is not what they thought it would be when they began. The process

Numerous problems remain which have not been touched upon here. A comprehensive analysis of these issues would need to consider, among other things, the problems raised by such phenomena as pure poetry and *Symboliste* poetry, as well as the dramatic monologue, in which there occurs a "disequilibrium," in Robert Langbaum's term, between the literal meaning of the speaker's statements and the ultimate meaning of the poem as a whole.[25] I would maintain that the conclusions advanced in this chapter are applicable even in these cases where poetry departs most obviously from explicit propositional assertion. To test this claim, however, would require a more extensive inquiry than I am prepared to undertake here. But even if one concedes that there is a kind of poetry which successfully circumvents logic and statement, the fact remains that this is not the case with all poetry. The theory which holds it to be the nature of poetry to refrain from assertion and argument is not supported by the facts.

---

by which a writer happens to arrive at his meaning, whether by strict deduction or by irrational inspiration or trance, does not provide a basis for conclusions about the logical and semantic status of the finished product.

25. *Poetry of Experience*, p. 72.

CHAPTER SIX

The Propositional Element in Poetry: Problems and Objections

Although the reader of the previous chapters may be willing to concede that antipropositional theories of poetry invite troublesome consequences, he may object that even more dire results are likely to follow from a theory which permits poetry to assert propositions. Despite the difficulties inherent in the several varieties of organic theory—and these difficulties are frequently acknowledged by organicists themselves—it is held that only such a theory can adequately account for our sense of the peculiar unity of form and content, thought and feeling, in a successful poem. In contrast, the theorist who maintains that poetry asserts propositions and argues hypotheses allegedly succumbs to most of the numerous heresies and fallacies in the contemporary critical lexicon: such a theorist commits the Didactic Heresy, the Heresy of Paraphrase, the Intentional Fallacy,[1] as well as the Form-Content

1. The "intentional fallacy" argument, as set forth in the well-known essay by W. K. Wimsatt and Monroe C. Beardsley (*The Verbal Icon* [Lexington: University of Kentucky Press, 1954], pp. 3–18) and endorsed by Brooks and other New Critics, is implied by the organicist principles discussed in Chapters One to Four. Since poetry asserts no

Dualism.[2] If we allow the poem to make a paraphrasable statement,

> we distort the relation of the poem to its "truth," we raise the problem of belief in a vicious and crippling form, we split the poem between its "form" and its "content"—we bring the statement to be conveyed into an unreal competition with science or philosophy or theology. . . . we misconceive the function of metaphor and meter.[3]

If we suppose that poems may assert propositions, we are left with no means of differentiating between poetry and nonpoetry and no means of protecting the poem from irrelevant doctrinal expectations. Propositional theory would seem to be no antidote at all for the confusions and inadequacies of the antipropositional approach.[4]

Form-Content Unity

Those who have promoted this negative view of what is entailed by a propositional theory, however, have taken much for granted in their understanding of "propositional dis-

---

statements and has no formulable "content," it is improper to speak of a meaning or content "intended" or "meant" by the poet. In effect, according to this view, the poet *must have no intention*, in the sense of a predetermined idea or emotion; the poem should generate itself out of its own internal laws. Authorial intention implies separable content and statement imposed upon the poem from "outside." For perceptive discussions of the relativistic and impressionistic implications of this doctrine, see Mark Spilka, "The Necessary Stylist: A New Critical Revision," in *Modern Criticism: Theory and Practice,* ed. Richard Foster and Walter Sutton (New York: Odyssey Press, 1963), pp. 328–34; and E. D. Hirsch, *Validity in Interpretation* (New Haven: Yale University Press, 1967).

2. The "form-content dualism . . . sees the poetic form as simply a superficial gilding of the content—not as something by which it is transformed" (Cleanth Brooks, "Literary Criticism: Poet, Poem, and Reader," in *Varieties of Literary Experience,* ed. Stanley Burnshaw [New York: New York University Press, 1962], p. 99).

3. *The Well Wrought Urn* (New York: Harcourt, Brace & Co., 1947), p. 184–85.

4. Representative statements of these objections may be found in *The Well Wrought Urn,* particularly in Chapter 11 and the concluding appendices, and in Murray Krieger, *The New Apologists for Poetry* (Minneapolis: University of Minnesota Press, 1956).

course." They tend to equate propositional with purely informational or scientific discourse, especially with respect to the separability of content and form. The content of a scientific proposition has a status which is independent of the particular symbols through which it happens to be expressed.[5] In contrast, any comparable alteration of the symbols of a poem changes the meaning of the poem. To hold that poems belong to the class of utterances which "say something," then, is apparently to succumb to the fallacy that the meaning of a poem, the "something," is detachable from the saying—as in the scientific statement—and from this error follow most of the heresies and fallacies catalogued above.

So the argument runs. But it is possible to make a distinction between propositional discourse and scientific or mathematical discourse. It is not difficult to find examples of expository writing in which the full meaning is closely bound up with the form. Consider the following sentence from J. L. Austin's *Sense and Sensibilia,* a posthumously published treatise which attacks the sense-data theories of A. J. Ayer. Austin is commenting on the beginning of Ayer's book: "In these paragraphs we already seem to see the plain man, here under the improbable aspect of Ayer himself, dribbling briskly into position in front of his own goal, and squaring up to encompass his destruction."[6] Since Austin is writing expository prose, I need have no reservations, I trust, in attributing a declarative content to his remarks. And yet I would hesitate to contend that the mode of expression could be altered without altering the full meaning of the sentence. On the contrary, much of the

---

5. For example, Boyle's Law of the expansion of gases may be expressed in a variety of forms without sacrificing the integrity of the concept. One may say: "The volume of a fixed quantity of gas varies inversely with the pressure if the temperature is constant," or, alternately, "$PV = K$," or "$P = \dfrac{K}{V}$," where the value of K depends upon the weight of the gas. Regardless of which *form* is employed, the content of meaning communicated—Boyle's Law itself—remains unaltered.

6. *Sense and Sensibilia,* ed. G. L. Warnock (Oxford: Clarendon Press, 1962), p. 6.

satiric point is a product of formal strategies: the witty analogy with the soccer player unaware that he is about to
score against his own team, the ironic implications of the
adverb "briskly," the effect of exaggeration conveyed by the
phrase, "to encompass his destruction," the rhetorical effect of
the syntax, which builds to a climax in that phrase, and so
forth. The style, in other words, invests the sentence with a
quality whose presence would be out of place in a scientific
treatise, a sense of the writer's feeling or attitude toward his
subject. This attitude is a real part of the *meaning* of the
sentence. If we translate the sentence into other words, we
weaken its ironic implications—or change them to something
else—and thus alter the character of what is said.

On the other hand, there is quite clearly a "paraphrasable
content" which can be abstracted from Austin's sentence. The
sentence *says* something like: "Ayer's argument, unbeknownst
to Ayer, is self-refuting." Such a paraphrase, if only an approximation, reproduces a portion of the whole meaning of the
utterance. To be sure, the paraphrase also omits a portion of
the whole meaning, namely, the ironic nuances which, as we
have seen, are communicated to a large extent through the
indirections of style. Thus we can say that Austin's statement
is on the one hand "unified," in that its style participates in its
full meaning, and that on the other hand it makes a "paraphrasable assertion" which constitutes a part, though not the whole,
of its total meaning.

I dwell on this example for this reason: if we were to adopt
such sentences as Austin's, rather than purely mathematical or
scientific propositions, as our paradigm of "propositional" or
"assertive" discourse, we would then be in a position to recognize a sense in which expository, paraphrasable assertions are
compatible with a type of "unified" relationship between the
constituent parts of the discourse. For Austin's sentence,
though it is propositional, is "unified" in that its form contrib-
utes to its total meaning. But if this is the case, then one of the
chief objections to a propositional poetics has been over-

thrown, for it is then possible for us to take an utterance as making a propositional assertion without our necessarily perpetrating a mechanical form-content dualism of the message-decoration type. If a nonpoetic sentence like Austin's may possess a unity of form and content even though it makes an assertion, why cannot the same be said of a poem?

But when we speak of "unified" utterances, there is another sense of this term which must be considered. Up to this point, we have been speaking of a "unified" utterance as one in which the form participates in and helps to shape the total meaning, so that this total meaning cannot be paraphrased without considerable reduction—that is, exclusion of the nuances and attitudes. But there is another type of relationship between content and form, that which has been earlier referred to as a ground-consequent relationship. If we recall once more that "form" implies as a correlative the emotions and attitudes it reflects, we can see that in a sense the "unity" of a particular utterance rests in the degree to which its form and the concommitant attitudes are actually grounded in, belong with, and are determined by the conceptual content. This relationship of "belonging with" is built into the conventions and usages of our speech and conduct, conventions which in turn are rooted in our world-views and values. Certain kinds of attitudes conventionally attach to certain kinds of conceptualizations, although the poet exercises a wide freedom in choosing which of the many possible conventions he will employ.

If we return for a moment to Austin's paradigm-sentence, we can see that the ironic attitude suggested by the various formal effects is connected with what the sentence says conceptually. That is, we recognize the suitability of the ironic tone because we know that an ironic attitude conventionally belongs with and follows from the kind of ideas which the statement expresses.[7] Style and attitude "follow from" concep-

7. The understanding of the operation of convention presented here is, I believe, compatible with the theory of "intrinsic genre" set forth by E. D. Hirsch in *Validity in Interpretation*, pp. 68–126. It might be thought

tual, descriptive content according to the conventions governing verbal communication. Of course there are numerous available conventions, and the writer's technique must determine which conventions are to be brought into play and which are to be excluded from a given context. For example, the descriptive, conceptual idea "Volpone is a rogue" may be developed in such a way as to emphasize potentially negative descriptive features (Volpone is dishonest, deceitful, lustful), positive ones (Volpone is vital, indefatigable, impulsive), or a combination of both. The point is that regardless of which particular descriptive features are emphasized in the context, the attitudes, pro or con, which are generated will be rooted in and will follow from those descriptive features. Attitudes are comprehensible only with respect to their prior conceptual grounds.[8] In Austin's sentence, the ironic attitude is grounded in a determinate set of negative features within the descriptive context —Ayer's self-destroying arguments—and thus the whole utterance passes the test of unity.

Were a reader ignorant of the convention according to which Austin's idea is the sort which justifies an ironic attitude, he would find Austin's tone inexplicably arch—the form and the content would appear dissociated. An actual dissociation occasionally occurs in freshman compositions, where the student conveys a tone of sarcasm or disapproval toward his subject but fails to indicate the grounds of his negative feelings. Another form of dissociation, in this case more calculated, is characteristic of advertising slogans and jingles. "Ultra-Brite entered my life—wow!" squeals the young lady in the toothpaste commercial. The emphatic style here is dissociated, being attached to a concept about which only an imbe-

---

that a theory which sees the relationship between concepts and feelings as "conventional" is incapable of accounting for poetic works which deviate from convention. But Hirsch demonstrates that this is not the case: see pp. 103–11.

8. Once more it is necessary to emphasize that the priority of the conceptual spoken of here does not entail any temporal priority during poetic composition.

cile could feel the excitement the style suggests. Of course we understand the convention whereby in advertisements enthusiasm is wildly disproportionate to its causes, but in such a case the convention is itself irrational, and we do not need to be taken in by it.

In my earlier discussion of Stevens' "The Course of a Particular," I argued that the propositional assertions made by the poem act as the grounds of the dramatically acted-out emotional response.[9] The conceptual clarity and seriousness of the speaker's estimate of his situation give the emotional and psychological attitudes their sensitivity and power. The internal coherence of the attitudes exists only with reference to their intentional objects, the state of affairs which they are "about," defined through the poem's propositional thrust. Every attempt to determine the propriety of specific formal devices will force the critic to consider the relationship between these devices and the poem's conceptual understanding of its subject. Consider the conclusion of the poem:

> The leaves cry. It is not a cry of divine attention,
> Nor the smoke-drift of puffed-out heroes, nor human cry.
> It is the cry of leaves that do not transcend themselves,
>
> In the absence of fantasia, without meaning more
> Than they are in the final finding of the ear, in the thing
> Itself, until, at last, the cry concerns no one at all.

The involved syntactical pattern of the final four lines is determined by the mood of emotional exhaustion and attrition which the syntax reflects. This mood is in turn rooted in the speaker's conceptual understanding of what his situation is. Because he *conceives* his situation as a world void of transcendent meaning, the propriety of his desolate tone and attitude is established; such an attitude follows as an intelligent and reasonable response to the situation. This assessment presupposes the existence of a convention which governs the relationship

9. See above, Chapter One, p. 30.

between the conception and the attitude; it also presupposes that an extrinsic criterion of propriety is permitted application. That is, we must be able to say that the convention whereby a tone of desolation or despair attaches to the protagonist's idea that objects "do not transcend themselves" is not arbitrary— that such deep and disturbing feelings are appropriate as human responses to the perception. Once the character of the conceptual content and the attitudes expressed through form have been determined by the critic, he must then invoke criteria which indicate, in general terms, what counts as a proper response to a situation like that of the poem; these criteria will have to come from the critic's own philosophical and ethical framework. Only in terms of this ground-consequent scheme with its governing extrinsic criteria can a critic differentiate between unified utterances like Stevens' and the bathos of the sentimental poem or the advertising slogan, where the obligation to state matters of trivial or no consequence in elevated and ecstatic tones results in the dissociation characteristic of inflated rhetoric. Our very ability to recognize such common literary sins as bathos and sentimentality, indeed our very ability to understand language, presupposes that an ideal of proportion between ground and consequent governs the relation between content and form and that there is an appeal to extrinsic human norms.

If I have labored this somewhat commonsensical theory excessively, it is because it constitutes a significant departure from the dominant trend of critical opinion in our period. The organicist, because he assumes that language should not be *about* experience but should embody experience itself in its immediacy, disapproves of the form-content distinction as inherently misleading and vicious when applied to poetry. When he speaks of a "unity of form and content," he is not interested in a mere connection or interrelation between discriminable entities, for it is the very notion of separable entities that the organicist cannot accept. From the point of view of the monistic theory espoused by such critics as Frye and Wheelwright, the form-content unity must be an *identity;* the very categories of form and content, like those of subject and object, mind and matter, language and reality, are misleading and must be superseded, since such dichotomies are based upon a rationalistic falsification of the seamless oneness of experience at the mythic level. Others, like Brooks, Krieger, and Wimsatt, less fully committed to this monistic position, nevertheless tend to conceive of poetic unity as a transcendental, nonrational identity, implicitly presupposing an identity of language and experience analogous to the mystery of the Christian Incarnation. Just as these critics were originally led to conclude that, because experience is a seamless and continuous "intensive manifold," poetry must not indulge in the rationalistic differentiations of propositional and logical language, so they attack the heresy of paraphrase and the form-content dualism on the ground that, because poetry is a seamless, organic unity, criticism cannot abide rationalistic distinctions.

The antipropositional theorist, by denying the priority of conceptual predication to dramatized attitude, by denying that conceptual content can even be distinguished from form and attitude, and by refusing to permit the "intrusion" of prior extrinsic standards governing propriety and reasonableness of response, destroys the ground-consequent relationship between content and form. Since a poem cannot assert anything or be *about* anything outside itself, there is no possibility of its dramatization of attitudes being "grounded" in anything but itself. The self-contained world of dramatized "experience," having been "freed" from its conceptual grounds, is about nothing but its own dissociated subjectivity. The *act* of discovery is forcibly severed from the *content* of discovery, and the unity of the poem is destroyed. We are thrown back upon the consequences of Richards' inversion of the priority of referential ground to emotion. That is, we are deprived, at least in theory, of the means which would permit us to distinguish between properly grounded and thus unified complexes of thought and feeling and the dissociation and bathos of the singing commercial.

It will be evident that the notion of "unity" of form and content advanced in the present chapter is not to be confused with a monistic identity or a transcendental unity. Form and content may exist in a harmonious, functional, and mutually reinforcing way, but they are not identical. If the aspects of discourse cannot be kept conceptually distinct, then we have no means of analyzing language, and criticism ceases to be an analytic discipline and becomes a form of inferior transcendentalist poetry. This is not to hold that a sharp line of demarcation can be drawn where conceptual content ends and form begins, where ideas cease and nuances, feelings, and attitudes take over. Indeed, it is difficult even to draw a clear boundary between such words as "ideas" on the one hand, and "feelings" and "attitudes" on the other, as is evidenced by the fact that these words are often used interchangeably. Another problem is raised by the fact that in most instances of language, the thoughts through which situations are objectified are themselves constituted by the forms of language in which the situation is viewed.[10] Neither the poet nor the ordinary speaker first conceives a preverbal idea and then casts about for a form to put it in, any more than the interpreter determines first what the ideas are and then afterward the form. But the fact that form and content are merged in a continuum does not invalidate the employment of a form-content distinction in criticism. In practice, not even organicist critics have been able to free themselves completely from "theme-treatment" distinctions in discussing particular poems. For even though earnest proclamations of the "inseparability" of the constituents of

10. John Casey has emphasized this point in his discussion of the Wittgensteinian concept of "seeing as" (*The Language of Criticism* [London: Methuen and Co., 1966], pp. 28–29 and *passim*). Casey's conclusions with respect to the proper way of dealing with the problem of form-content unity differ sharply from those expressed in this work.

poetic meaning are not difficult to make—especially when such locutions as "unity" and "inseparable" are permitted to remain unanalyzed—it is hard to see how such proclamations can be substantiated once the very categories of which the unity is composed are repudiated. For our understanding·of the concept of unity of discourse depends upon our entertaining a "dualistic" distinction between the entities which are held to be unified. It is only when we have specified the distinguishable entities which are to be joined that we are in a position to comprehend the unity.

The Heresy of Paraphrase

The problem of paraphrasability in poetry has been the occasion of much confusion in contemporary poetic theory. One major cause of the confusion has been the fact that of the many critics who have argued that poetic meaning is "unparaphrasable," none have specified the conditions of paraphrasability. That is, it may be true to say that a poem cannot be paraphrased, but as long as one neglects to say just what constitutes "paraphrasability," the statement will amount to little more than a truism. Many of the utterances made in ordinary, nonpoetic discourse are "unparaphrasable," in that any paraphrase that is offered will inevitably leave out or distort some aspect of their meaning. It helps little, then, to say that poetry is unparaphrasable, for, in a sense, most instances of language are also. Yet it would be absurd to hold that most utterances are unparaphrasable. The problem lies in our expectations regarding what a paraphrase should do. If we expect a paraphrase to reproduce an equivalent or completely synonymous reformulation of the *total* meaning of the original, then very few sentences (only those wholly devoid of emotional nuance, in fact) can be regarded as paraphrasable. But if the aim of a paraphrase is more modestly conceived as giving an equivalent not of the total meaning of the utterance paraphrased but only of the *conceptual* portion of that meaning, then we can speak of most utterances as accessible to paraphrase. According to this usage, to ascribe paraphrasability to an utterance is not to say that the paraphrase exhausts the full meaning, for there is still an area of meaning of which the paraphrase will give little or no account. Within this understanding of the term, it seems proper to hold that poems are paraphrasable: we can reproduce, to a large degree at least, their conceptual content.

Those who reject propositional theories of poetry often assume that any theory which allows poetry to make assertions inevitably commits the heresy of paraphrase, that is, takes the meaning of the poem to be equivalent to its paraphrastic reduction, a step which reduces form to the status of superfluous decoration laid upon an independent content. However, as we have just seen, it is not necessary to regard total equivalence as a condition of paraphrasability; in fact, such an expectation leads to the absurdity whereby almost all ordinary non-poetic statements become unparaphrasable. If we hold that a poem asserts something, we are not obliged to hold that its total meaning is contained in what it asserts, that is, in that conceptual content which can be reproduced by paraphrase. We can still recognize other important aspects of the total meaning, particularly those aspects of which I have spoken as dramatized or acted out in the poem. If a propositional theory *were* obliged to equate the meaning of the poem with a paraphrasable "message," the objections would be legitimate. The old message-decoration theory *did* assume the synonymy of the "matter" with its paraphrase and reduced form to mere superadded ornament. The service performed by contemporary organicists in laying this pernicious theory to rest should be applauded, but the logical status of propositional theory in principle is not jeopardized by the deficiencies of certain historical versions of the theory. Under the conditions specified above, the analytic abstraction of an asserted content from a poem may be undertaken without betraying the principle that the total meaning of the poem is a synthesis of conceptual and attitudinal meanings, that propositional and formal constituents are unified.

But what happens to those aspects of meaning omitted by the paraphrase? As I have indicated, such problems are by no means peculiar to the analysis of poetic meaning but complicate the analysis of nonpoetic meaning as well. If we look once again at Austin's sentence, which served as a typical case, we find a set of ironic nuances which would appear to elude paraphrase. These ironic nuances, although they cannot be paraphrased, can nevertheless be *described*, as I describe them here by labeling them "ironic." Whereas a paraphrase purports to reproduce a meaning synonymous with the conceptual portion of the original, a description attempts rather to give information *about* the aspects of meaning which are its objects. Descriptions do not seek to reproduce their objects. Thus when I describe Austin's tone as "ironic," or when I elaborate this description, I make a conceptual statement about the utterance, but I do not claim that my description in any way stands for or reproduces a content present in the original the way a paraphrase does. A description of something as "ironic" does not reproduce the actual quality of irony in the object. The concept of a description, as distinguished from a paraphrase, is helpful for it opens up a wide area of poetic meaning which cannot be reproduced by critical reformulation but which is still accessible to analysis.

In short, then, the total meaning of a poem can be paraphrased and described, but it cannot be *fully reproduced* in any formulation but the poem itself. Even if a critic were to adduce an exhaustive paraphrase of a poem's propositional content and a complete description of every nuance of every attitude, he would not have infringed on the territory of the poet nor obviated the need for him to write his poem. For the descriptive portion of his analysis would remain only a statement *about* the complexity and particularity of the poem's enacted attitudes. The description, however useful in facilitating our entry into the poem, would remain a description and not the object itself. The advantages of the position taken here are twofold: on the one hand, this view makes the poem accessible to critical reformulation and interpretation whereas organicism, in principle at least, does not. We saw in Chapter Four that the logical implication of Brooks's theory is a total discontinuity between the paraphrase and the poem itself, a conclusion which leads to impressionism and relativism. On the other hand, the theory advanced here does not allow the critical paraphrase or interpretation to become a substitute for the poem—the defect of the message-decoration theory. The theory assigns due authority to interpretation without allowing interpretation to swallow the poem.

Belief and Propriety

If poetry does assert, it is only natural that belief in, or assent to the truth of, what it asserts should be a relevant consideration in estimating poetic value. As we saw in Chapter Four, such a theory as Brooks's, even though hostile in principle to the application of criteria dependent upon belief and truth of correspondence, itself presupposes the relevance of such criteria in its appeal to maturity, tough-mindedness, and other ethical norms. Even in the extreme organicism of Frye, according to which the imagination is "totally" its own law, we find a demand for an "educated imagination" a reluctance to see literature as purely a "wish-fulfillment dream," and thus an implicit concession to the importance of truth and belief. In short, the slightest gesture toward bringing the poem into relation with external reality presupposes the acceptance of the criteria of belief and correspondence, however much this acceptance may be obscured by ominous warnings and disclaimers. It is therefore unfair to suppose that only a propositional theory invites the problem of belief. Any theory not wholly willing to divorce the poem from the real world presumes the relevance of belief and invites the problem of belief no less.

One reason for the reluctance of theorists to accept belief-criteria, or to own up to the presence of them in their own theories, is the fear of rendering criticism hopelessly impressionistic and relativistic. For it is asked, how can belief be regarded as a necessary constituent of appreciation in a period in which beliefs are not universally shared? The question, however, is logically irrelevant to the issue of the validity of a propositional theory, since the problem of disagreement in critical opinions is in no way a peculiar liability of propositional theory. It is possible for critics to differ just as violently over whether or not a poem has coherence, complexity, organic wholeness, or aesthetic harmony, as over whether or not it is true. Indeed, if the problem of impressionism and relativism is to be raised, then one may speculate that the denial of the presence of assertion in poetry and the refusal to allow the poem's statements to be tested against external reality are more likely to encourage than to eliminate a climate of disagreement. For in discarding the appeal to external reality, we discard one of the chief sources of the critic's appeal to the common experiences of his readers.

But regardless of the consequences, the critic will find it almost impossible to make normative judgments without appealing outside the poem to his own beliefs and presuppositions about reality. Instead of indulging in useless complaints about the relativity of such beliefs, or futile warnings against the introduction of external philosophical and moral commitments, the critic would do better to see to it that the beliefs and commitments he must inevitably bring to his reading are as flexible, intelligent, and comprehensive as possible. The crude and barbaric application of dogma to poetry is always a danger to be avoided in criticism. The way to avoid it, however, is not by contriving theories which evade the problem of belief by trying to see to it that it cannot arise, but rather by accepting the problem as a problem and doing one's best to refine one's beliefs and avoid rigidity in their application. The problem of belief, after all, is not a problem which plagues the literary critic alone. A greater degree of uniformity in poetic judgments is not likely to come about until a comparable uniformity is achieved in philosophy, ethics, politics, and religion. The problem of belief arises constantly in everyday experience, where we are forced to choose between beliefs, to accept or reject the beliefs of another; there is no good reason why this problem should be thought inappropriate when it rears its head in the criticism of poetry.

The negative side of the problem of belief may be illustrated by an examination of Ralph Waldo Emerson's poem, "Brahma":

> If the red slayer think he slays,
>   Or if the slain think he is slain,
> They know not well the subtle ways
>   I keep, and pass, and turn again.
>
> Far or forgot to me is near;
>   Shadow and sunlight are the same,
> The vanished gods to me appear;
>   And one to me are shame and fame.
>
> They reckon ill who leave me out;
>   When me they fly, I am the wings;
> I am the doubter and the doubt,
>   And I the hymn the Brahmin sings.
>
> The strong gods pine for my abode,
>   And pine in vain the sacred Seven;
> But thou, meek lover of the good!
>   Find me, and turn thy back on heaven.[11]

The poem asserts the Hindu doctrine of Unity, emphasizing the illusory nature of evil and separation. The victim of "the red slayer" may think he is being murdered, but only because he fails to realize that he and the slayer are one, a fact which would presumably afford him a degree of consolation. He who doubts the doctrine is similarly deluded, for his very doubt is a part of the universal whole.

11. *Selected Prose and Poetry*, 2d ed., ed. Reginald Cook (New York: Holt, Rinehart & Winston, 1969), p. 486.

Let us imagine a reader or critic who finds himself unable to take these ideas seriously. He feels that Emerson's merging of the identities of the slayer and his victim falsifies human experience. The reader's reservations about the intellectual substance of the poem, I would maintain, cannot be kept out of his assessment of the poem as a whole. For if the stylistic-emotional aspects of a poem are grounded in the poem's conceptualization, then, to the degree this conceptualization is unacceptable, the stylistic-emotional response will be to some degree vitiated. In the present instance, the poem's stylistic-emotional posture is elevated and portentous. It draws attention to itself, signalling to the reader that weighty matters are involved. But since our reader is unable to take the poem's statement about these matters seriously[12] as an understanding of reality, the elevation and portentousness of manner become for him mere bathos. The case is similar to the example described by Richards, where "a commonplace, either of thought or feeling, is delivered with an air appropriate to a fresh discovery or a revelation,"[13] except that in this instance the thought is not so much "commonplace" in the eye of our reader as preposterous. A line like "I am the doubter and the

12. There is, of course, a difference between not being able to "take seriously" an idea or argument and not being convinced of its truth or actively believing it. Terms like "disbelief" and "failure of assent" cover a broad range of mental dispositions from an active repulsion to a state that is noncommittal and neutral. It is difficult to say how far a reader must be *actively* committed to the beliefs expressed by a poem as a precondition for the fullest appreciation, but I would argue that the reader must, at a minimum, see the ideas as at least intelligent, at least not stupid or preposterous. If the ideas seem without any validity as ideas whatsoever, it is difficult to see how one could appreciate the poem with any wholeness of mind. As Erich Heller puts it:

There are ideas and beliefs so prosaic, outlandish or perverse in their innermost structure that no great or good poetry can come from them: for instance, Hitler's racialism. It is this *negative* consideration that to me finally proves the intimate *positive* relation between belief, thought and poetry. If there were no relation, there would be no reason either why the most perverse or idiotic beliefs should not be convertible into *great* poetry. They are not (*The Disinherited Mind* [New York: Farrar, Straus and Cudahy, 1957], p. 159 n).

13. *Practical Criticism* (New York: Harcourt, Brace & Co., 1935), p. 207.

doubt," rhetorically impressive as it is outside its context, remains effective only so long as our reader is able to ignore what it means. To the extent that he is capable of compartmentalizing his responses, the reader will appreciate the rhetorical grandeur of the line. But if he judges the line as part of a total poetic act of the mind, an act both conceptual and emotional, the intellectual inadequacy of its statement will prevent him from enjoying the fullest kind of poetic response.

The pragmatist can be expected to object that if our reader's requirements are so stringent as to deprive him of the ability to enjoy the poem, then he would do well to discard them for the sake of the added pleasure he can gain. The reader should set aside his merely intellectual reservations and give himself up to the "imaginative possibility" represented by the poem—that ecstatic state of mind in which the slayer and the slain *are* one and the same—accepting as *poetically* if not empirically true that which is, in Empson's phrase, true within the imagined "world of experience" of the poem itself. Thus we would achieve the "wider sympathies" and "greater tolerance" which Frye defines as the aim of reading. But this sort of objection only returns us to our familiar problem: read under the conditions prescribed by Empson and Frye, what poem would not be judged perfect? Must we ask no questions about the claims of a pleasure and a sympathy which is purchased at the expense of surrendering our critical faculties? As Harvey Breit has written, "pleasure derived from the suppression of the intelligence is diluted pleasure very much akin to dissipation."[14] Unless it is assumed that all attitudes and world-views are equally valid, we are forced to take a critical look at the ideas stated by poems, and to take such a critical look is to risk the possibility of our not agreeing with what we find. It will not do to say that ideas do not matter in poetry because, as George Boas says, "the ideas in poetry are usually stale and often false . . . ," for such a view often derives from excessive and un-

14. Quoted by Marvin Laser and Norman Fruman, eds., *Studies in J. D. Salinger* (New York: Odyssey Press, 1963), pp. 13–14.

critical admiration for poems made out of stale and false ideas.[15]

Ideas do matter in poetry, but no one could seriously hold that a poem is authenticated solely by virtue of the soundness of the ideas which inform it. A fatuous thesis will weaken a well-written poem, but a sound argument will not redeem a piece of doggerel. In short, a minimal degree of truth and soundness is a necessary but not a sufficient criterion of poetic value.[16] Thus the verification of a poem's propositional content is only an initial step in the critical process; more crucial—and more difficult to perform—is the evaluation of the dramatized psychological and emotional attitudes, whose character is reflected through style. Once the conceptual grounds of these attitudes have been verified, questions of the propriety and adequacy of the dramatized response come into play. The critic then turns to the question of whether the attitudes are intelligent and humanly sound, that is, whether the attitudes follow in a relevant manner from the conceptualizations and whether they are adequate to them. The question now is not

15. Quoted by René Wellek and Austin Warren, *Theory of Literature*, 3d ed. (New York: Harcourt, Brace & World, 1962), p. 110. This is not to say that the reader or critic should be unwilling to allow his preconceived beliefs to be themselves modified or changed through their collision with the poet's beliefs. Reading *critically* means not only criticizing poetry against one's own standards, but having the tact and flexibility to examine those standards critically from the point of view of the poem. The good critic will, without surrendering to a wholly uncritical "tolerance," attempt to recognize when he is applying merely willful and arbitrary standards and will permit an interplay between his own standards and values and those embodied within the poem.

16. The kind of truth to which I am referring is a general, philosophical truth rather than an accuracy to specific fact. It may be noted, however, that there are instances where even factual accuracy may be required in a poem. Shakespeare's "Seacoast of Bohemia" is a harmless error, but there are contexts in which comparable literal inaccuracy is destructive to the effect of the poem. Consider, for instance, Yeats's lines in "Among School Children":

> Plato thought nature but a spume that plays
> Upon a ghostly paradigm of things . . .

Imagine what the effect on the poem would be if for "Plato" one were to substitute "Bacon" or "Carnap."

how truly the poet conceives or defines his situation, but how intelligently and maturely he responds to that conception.

The difference between good and bad poetry lies not only in the superiority of the good poem's conceptual understanding of its subject, but in large part in the good poet's ability to respond adequately, stylistically and emotionally, with respect to his conceptualization. The lesser poet may frequently assert an intelligent idea, but he lacks either the linguistic or the emotional resources to respond adequately to the idea. This kind of difference can be roughly illustrated by juxtaposing a series of passages of varying quality in which an approximately similar conceptual statement about a subject is made. The first two passages are from Shelley, the third is a complete poem translated by Ralegh, the fourth an excerpt from William Carlos Williams:

> They die—the dead return not. Misery
>   Sits near an open grave and calls them over,
> A youth with hoary hair and haggard eye.
>   They are the names of kindred, friends, and lover,
> Which he so feebly calls; they are all gone—
> Fond wretch, all dead! those vacant names alone,
>   This most familiar scene, my pain,
>   These tombs,—alone remain.
>
> > Shelley, "Death," 1817

> First our pleasures die—and then
> Our hopes, and then our fears—and when
> These are dead, the debt is due,
> Dust claims dust—and we die too.
>
> > Shelley, "Death," 1820

> The sun may set and rise;
> But we, contrariwise,
> Sleep after our short light
> One everlasting night.
>
> > Ralegh, translation of Catullus

He's come out of the man
and he's let
the man go—
          the liar

Dead
     his eyes
rolled up out of
the light—a mockery
          which
love cannot touch—

just bury it
and hide its face—
for shame.
    William Carlos Williams, "Death"[17]

In saying that these four statements about the dreadfulness and
finality of death are "approximately" synonymous in conceptual content, I am glossing over important respects in which
their arguments differ. But the most noteworthy differences in
the passages are differences of style and attitude rather than of
intellectual outlook. The emotional response to the idea of
death and its finality in the Shelley passages is hysterical and
crude by comparison with the responses conveyed by Ralegh
and Williams. The discontinuous and broken syntax of the first
passage and the use of the melodramatic personification of
"Misery" suggest a violent and distracted emotional state
whose predominant character is that of a somewhat conventional self-pity and anguish. Passage two is more subdued, but
the monotonous trochaic singsong and the obviously padded
diction ("and then . . . and then") combine to vulgarize and
enfeeble the emotional attitude. Both passages are clumsy in

17. *The Complete Poetical Works of Percy Bysshe Shelley*, ed.
Thomas Hutchinson (London: Oxford University Press, 1934), pp. 546,
622; *English Renaissance Poetry*, ed. John Williams (Garden City,
N. Y.: Vintage Books, 1963), p. 133; *The Collected Earlier Poems of
William Carlos Williams* (New York: New Directions, 1951), p. 79.

execution and as a consequence convey a relatively insensitive response to the subject, even though the conceptual statement is respectable enough. The Ralegh poem, although admittedly very slight, achieves a blunt, subdued solemnity through the use of plain diction and syntax, terse monosyllables, and the strategic placement of the word "contrariwise." Superficially considered, the first passage from Shelley is more "dramatic" than the Ralegh poem in the sense that it possesses greater immediacy—a sense that the action is taking place spontaneously in the mind without abstract mediation. But Ralegh's lines, although overtly mediated by thought, are richer in truly dramatic power—the sense of an authentic and engaged personality behind the speech—than is Shelley's overemphatic and stereotyped anguish. The Williams lines possess the immediacy of Shelley's but inform it with a bitterness of tone more intense than Ralegh's. The syntax is disjunctive and asymmetrical, but not haphazardly so. The line and word arrangement is suggestive of subtle emphases of meaning and feeling. By breaking the line in irregular and unexpected fashion, Williams suggests a sense of the speaker's inability to come to terms with the unfathomable fact represented by the corpse, yet the precise colloquial bluntness of diction ("just bury it") prevents the attitude from degenerating into mere distraction and hysteria. The harshness and callousness apparently directed toward the dead man ("the liar") is really directed at death itself and is a veil for a subtle compassion.

This comparison, though it oversimplifies the problem, may serve to indicate broadly the way in which stylistic judgments are ultimately implicated in questions of intellectual and ethical value. Because of the intentional character of style and emotional attitude, stylistic defects like Shelley's stereotyped diction and insensitive metric are finally lapses in perceptivity and insight (not necessarily on the part of the poet himself, with whom we are not concerned, but in the poem). Notice that in labeling Shelley's diction "stereotyped," we imply not only an "aesthetic" weakness but an ethical failing as well. It is worth calling attention to the significant fact that many of the common terms employed in criticizing verbal style—"pretentious," "banal," "cliché," etc.—possess a double character, referring to lapses not only in technique but in intellectual and emotional sensitivity. Judgments of ethical decorum, then, are not performed subsequent to and apart from judgments of aesthetic technique and added on to them but are vital constituents of aesthetic judgments themselves. A poetic syllable, a word, a metaphor, represents a commitment to a stance, a choice of a position risked by the poet and by the critic who evaluates his poem. This is perhaps what T. S. Eliot meant when he said that "the author of a work of imagination is trying to affect us wholly, as human beings, whether he knows it or not; and we are affected by it as human beings, whether we intend to or not."[18]

18. *Selected Essays* (New York: Harcourt, Brace & World, 1950), p. 348. See also M. H. Abrams' essay, "Belief and the Suspension of Disbelief," in *Literature and Belief*, English Institute Essays, 1957, ed. M. H. Abrams (New York: Columbia University Press, 1958), p. 28. Abrams argues that no poet can "win our imaginative consent to the aspects of experience he presents" as long as he evades his "responsibility to the beliefs and prepossessions of our common experience, common sense, and common moral consciousness."
Some other theorists who have urged the relevance of belief in a manner congenial to my argument, without necessarily agreeing with me or with each other on most issues, are as follows: Yvor Winters, *In Defense of Reason* (Denver: Alan Swallow, 1947); *The Function of Criticism* (Denver: Alan Swallow, 1957); *Forms of Discovery* (Denver and Chicago: Alan Swallow, 1967). (See also my discussion of Winters' theory, pp. 162–65.) Wayne C. Booth, *The Rhetoric of Fiction* (Chicago: University of Chicago Press, 1961), pp. 118–47. Walter Sutton, "The Contextualist Dilemma—or Fallacy?" *Journal of Aesthetics and Art Criticism*, XVII (December, 1958), 219–29. Henry David Aiken, "The Aesthetic Relevance of Belief," *Aesthetic Inquiry*, ed. Monroe C. Beardsley and Herbert K. Schueller (Belmont, Calif.: Dickenson Publishing Co., 1967), pp. 141–54. J. V. Cunningham, *Tradition and Poetic Structure* (Denver: Alan Swallow, 1960). Morris Weitz, *Philosophy of the Arts* (Cambridge: Harvard University Press, 1950), pp. 134–52; *Philosophy and Literature* (Detroit: Wayne State University Press, 1963). Walter Stein, *Criticism as Dialogue* (Cambridge: Cambridge University Press, 1969). Edgar Wind, *Art and Anarchy* (New York: Vintage Books, 1969), pp. 52–67.
For a further discussion of the problem of belief, see Appendix A.

Modern and Classical Decorum

The concept of poetic decorum advanced above is a restatement of the ancient classical principle which Plato enunciated in the *Republic,* when he said that poetic style ought to be "appropriate to a life of courage and self-control."[19] Sir Philip Sidney's formulation in the *Defense of Poesy* is one of the most succinct statements of the principle:

> . . . the senate of poets hath chosen verse as their fittest raiment, . . . not speaking, table-talk fashion, or like men in a dream, words as they chanceably fall from the mouth, but peizing each syllable of each word by just proportion, according to the dignity of the subject.[20]

In good poetry, "each syllable" carries an emotional weight that is of precisely the proper degree of intensity—"just proportion"—in relation to the "dignity" or importance of the subject, as the subject is understood and defined by the poet. The theory presupposes a propositional content in the poem, a conceptualized definition of the subject, yet it makes allowance for the crucial influence of form in the full exploitation of that content. The theory specifies an internal connection be-

19. *The Republic of Plato,* ed. and trans. F. M. Cornford (New York: Oxford University Press, 1954), p. 88.
20. *The Defense of Poesy,* ed. Albert S. Cook (Boston: Ginn and Co., 1890), p. 11. In classical poetics, this concept of decorum with respect to *subject* appears in conjunction with two other types of decorum: decorum with respect to *genre* and *character.* This latter type, applied chiefly to narrative and dramatic poetry, specifies that style must be suited to the dramatic speaker's personality, social class status, etc. (Ben Jonson invokes this concept in his conversation with Drummond when he says that Sir Philip Sidney "did not keep a decorum in making everyone speak as well as himself.") This concept is the prototype of the modern principle of dramatic propriety, and is inadequate for criticism of the lyric for reasons given above, Chapter Four, pp. 98–99. The concept of decorum with respect to genre is bound up with the classical doctrine of the three levels of style, the "low" style, for instance, being thought suitable for satire. The concept of levels of style is a logical extension of the theory that style is suited to the "dignity of the subject."

tween conceptual understanding and the human attitudes which properly attach to that understanding.

At certain points in his famous critique of Wordsworth's poetry in the *Biographia*, Coleridge implicitly adheres to the Sidneyan principle of decorum rather than to the dramatic principle implied by his own organic theory. In objecting to the "mental bombast" of the "Intimations Ode"—"thoughts and images too great for the subject"—Coleridge assumes the necessity of an adequate conceptual subject as a prior ground of the emotional response. Wordsworth "affects an intensity of feeling disproportionate to such knowledge and value of the objects described, as can be anticipated of men in general . . ." It is clearly not sufficient mitigation for Coleridge that Wordsworth's disproportionate intensity is dramatically plausible and "in character." Coleridge's withering critique of Wordsworth's rhapsodic comparison of the child to a philosopher and prophet involves an "intrusion" of empirical standards of truth and falsity: "Children at this age give no such information of themselves."[21] These criticisms are incompatible with Coleridgean organicism, as I. A. Richards was quick to perceive when he scolded Coleridge for "laboring in such a trough of literalism" here.[22]

In our own period, the classical concept of decorum has received its sharpest restatement in the theory of Yvor Winters:

> The business of the poet can be stated simply. The poet deals with human experience in words. Words are symbols of concepts, which have acquired connotations of feeling in addition to their denotation of concept. The poet, then, as a result of the very nature of his medium, must make a rational statement about an experience, and as rationality is a part of the medium, the ultimate value of the poem will

21. *Complete Works*, ed. W. T. G. Shedd (New York: Harper & Brothers, 1853), III, 477–82.
22. *Coleridge on Imagination* (New York: W. W. Norton & Co., 1950), p. 136.

depend in a fair measure on the soundness of the rationality: it is possible, of course, to reason badly, just as it is possible to reason well. But the poet is deliberately employing the connotative content of language as well as the denotative: so that what he must do is make a rational statement about an experience, at the same time employing his language in such a manner as to communicate the emotion which ought to be communicated by that rational understanding of the particular subject. In so far as he is able to do this, the poem will be good; in so far as the subject itself is important, the poem will be great.[23]

Words communicate feelings, Winters says, "by virtue of their conceptual identity, and in so far as this identity is impaired they will communicate less of these and communicate them with less force and precision."[24] More thoroughly than Sidney or the ancient classical theorists, Winters' formulation clarifies the way in which the emotions which "ought to be communicated" in connection with a particular conceptual understanding are fused into a total statement through the operations of poetic diction, imagery, syntax, and meter. Winters' concept of the "morality of poetry," a morality which he sees to be as much a function of form as of propositional content, restates the essence of the classical synthesis. And in his analyses of such poems as Stevens' "Sunday Morning" and Valéry's *Ebauche d'un serpent*,[25] Winters rejuvenates the traditional categories by adapting them to wholly modern contexts of subject matter and feeling.

Winters' unconventional and unpopular evaluations of particular poets have often distracted attention from the importance of his theoretical contribution. In my opinion, no other contemporary theorist has come closer than Winters to resolv-

23. *Function of Criticism*, pp. 160–61.
24. *Ibid.*, pp. 103–4.
25. *In Defense of Reason*, pp. 441–43; *Function of Criticism*, pp. 63–74. See also the essay "Poetic Styles Old and New," in *A Celebration of Poets*, ed. Don Cameron Allen (Baltimore: Johns Hopkins Press, 1967), pp. 44–75.

ing age-old theoretical dichotomies and setting up a workable and comprehensive framework for evaluation. Winters sees poetry as a form of expository statement: "The short poem . . . is not essentially imitative or narrative, but expository." "The short poem is not an imitation of action." "The important thing is not action in itself, but the understanding of action."[26] But although Winters frequently seems to denigrate the dramatic principle, in truth what he objects to is not the dramatic as such, but the dramatic when it is cut off from an integrating framework of rational and moral understanding— i.e., mere action or experience presented for its own sake. In praising Valéry's *Ebauche d'un serpent*, Winters makes clear that what he is aiming at is not the exclusion of the dramatic but the fusion of the dramatic with the expository:

> The structure of the poem is that of a closely controlled development by association. . . . There is nothing resembling the free association of Pound's *Cantos;* but we have rather an imitation of the psychological movement of a great mind back and forth among closely related topics, the shifts occurring as the passion aroused by one topic suggests an aspect of another topic. . . . Valéry . . . is able . . . to borrow something from the dramatic method and something from the associationists, without sacrificing the essential form of the short poem, that of exposition, or its essential virtue, the most intelligent writing possible.[27]

Winters says that Valéry inherited "the extraordinary sensitivity to sensory perception" of such poets as Mallarmé and Rimbaud, "but he was not satisfied with it in a pure state. In Valéry we have this heightened sensory awareness, and we have the tone which convinces us that the details have meaning; but we also have the meaning, and the meaning is of quite as fine a quality as the rest."[28] That is, the poet presents an intellectually serious content as a ground, or, in Winters'

26. *Function of Criticism*, pp. 60–61.
27. *Ibid.*, p. 66.
28. *Ibid.*, pp. 68–69.

terms, a "motive" for the enactment of response. The *process* and the *content* of thought, which antipropositional theorists drive apart in spite of themselves, are here reconciled.

The reconciliation is possible because Winters presumes a functional connection between the poet's intellectual understanding of his subject and his feelings and style, between conceptual knowledge and emotional evaluation. It is only on the basis of this presupposition, according to Winters, that criticism becomes possible, since the propriety of style and emotion, of dramatic enactment, must always be referred back to the human importance of the subject. Thus Winters is able to define a model of unified discourse in which feeling is ideally proportional to motivating understanding and in which deviations from this unity such as sentimental and exaggerated feelings may be measured and judged. It is easy enough to reject Winters' argument on the grounds that no one can any longer presume to say what emotions "ought" to be motivated by a particular analysis of a situation, that is, on the grounds that there is no such thing as a "rational" response to a subject. But those who have made this objection have yet to demonstrate an alternative standard which does not covertly rely on precisely those assumptions which are said to have been discredited.

In classical decorum the propriety of style and attitude is determined with reference to the poet's idea of the "dignity of the subject." The assumption is that judgments of "dignity" must inevitably be made by the poet, that they are part of the inescapable business of poet and critic. But as conceptual predication comes to be thought of as alien to poetry, the relevance of such extrinsic judgments becomes questionable. The connection between conceptualization and emotional response, between the objective understanding of the subject and the poetic style, the ground-consequent connection which was the basis of the classical theory of decorum, is destroyed. We are forced back upon the contextual concept of decorum, Brooks's principle of dramatic propriety with its inherent circularity.

The principle of dramatic propriety represents an attempt to side-step extrinsic judgment by referring the propriety of style and attitude back to the unmediated experience presented in the poem itself, as if conceptualization could somehow be circumvented and as if experience could somehow be its own justification. It would be unfair and inaccurate to suggest that critics who invoke dramatic propriety are advocates of romantic irrationalism or of intensity for its own sake. But because dramatic theory lacks any principle capable of determining the proper degree of emotional intensity in a given context, the theory is open to the same objections which apply to the most relativistic and uncritical irrationalism. The dramatic principle can require the poet to do no more than speak "table talk fashion or like men in a dream," the latter being precisely what some of the more extreme mythopoeic critics claim the poet does.

Just as internal coherence depends upon and is subsumed by external correspondence, dramatic propriety must be subsumed by classical propriety if critical judgments are to be given a secure foundation. The combination of the two principles provides a completeness in criticism which cannot be achieved by dramatic propriety alone. Many, unfortunately, are likely to be repelled by the adjective "classical," with its present-day connotation of narrowness and restriction. But the classical principle of propriety is broad and flexible enough to be applicable to a radically unclassical conception of the human situation, and it is capable of embracing good poetry of all periods. The principle is still valid in an age which conceives experience as elusive and problematical, for even that view finally depends upon rational categories for its formulation. If the normative aspects of the principle depend heavily upon such ethically-weighted terms as "dignity," soundness, and maturity, they do so no less than alternative theories, in which the ultimate ethical commitments tend to be either concealed or in conflict with the theory itself.

Poetry and Nonpoetry

Up to this point, most of what has been said of poetry holds true of ordinary prose discourse as well: the propositional and logical character of poetry, its use of "enactment" grounded in conceptual predication, the norms of truth and propriety to which it is subject for validation, its fusion of content and form. If these pages have given disproportionate emphasis to the similarities between poetry and nonpoetic discourse, the excuse is that the balance has of late been tipped heavily toward the view that these two modes of writing are absolutely antithetical. It may be worthwhile to remember that poetry, after all, is finally a means of saying something, of getting something across to someone else. Whatever transformations the poetic imagination may work upon language, it is still language that is being employed, and the common properties of language are not subject to unlimited modification and metamorphosis.

But how, then, does poetry differ from nonpoetry? If poetry resembles prose by making statements, and if prose resembles poetry by expressing attitudes, and if both prose and poetry aim at the same *kind* of meaning, what is their point of differentiation? In my view, the distinguishing property of a poem is its highly developed and systematic employment of rhythm, a property which is inherent in the medium of verse. Although rhythm is present in all speech, it is much more fully articulated and systematized in poetry, and this is true of free as well as metrical verse. Even the loosest, most relaxed free verse is written in periodic elements of some kind and thus possesses a pattern of tempo and movement which is more emphatic, intense, and suggestive of emotional states than are the patterns found in prose. Rhythm, in conjunction with the conceptual powers of language, suggests attitudes which participate in the meaning of the whole. Although this participation of rhythm and meaning occurs in prose, the connection is even more intimate in poetry.

In his *Sound and Form in Modern Poetry*, Harvey Gross presents an account of the function of prosody which is, I believe, congenial to the present theory. Gross sees it as the business of prosody to "communicate states of awareness, tensions, emotions, all of man's inner life which the helter-skelter of ordinary propositional language cannot express."[29] Gross does not, however, as this statement might appear to imply, deny propositional content to poetry: prosody, he says, "develops out of . . . conceptual meaning. . . . A poem's prosody cannot exist apart from its propositional sense. Prosodic rhythm and propositional sense work as identities in poetic language. Phonetic patterning creates meaning in language; rhythm in linguistic structure is itself *sense*."[30] In poetry, Gross suggests, the psychological attitudes and nuances of meaning which can only be dramatized in "helter-skelter" fashion by the crude and random rhythms of ordinary prose are precisely correlated with the conceptual content to produce a unique identification of concept and feeling.

As Gross says, the rhythm of a verbal statement is itself a kind of "sense." The meaning of a poetic statement is always to some degree influenced by the fact that it is expressed in rhythmical form. It does not follow from this fact that such influence must invalidate or negate the declarative force of the poem or turn the poem into something that does not make a conceptual statement, even though the effect of rhythm is to complicate and extend the meaning of the whole statement to a large degree. It is true that there are instances in which rhythmical tensions may work strongly against the argumentative thrust of a poem. Normally, however, rhythmic tension does not run counter to conceptual content in a clear-cut and decisive manner. More commonly, the modification is indirect,

29. *Sound and Form in Modern Poetry* (Ann Arbor: University of Michigan Press, 1964), p. 10.
30. *Ibid.*, p. 17.

as when a poem rejects an idea or way of life while betraying in its rhythmic tone and its diction a longing or nostalgia for that which is being rejected. Quite as commonly rhythm works to fortify and intensify conceptual content, not to undercut it.

But however the rhythm may operate in a given instance, it is its presence, built into the poetic medium, as a systematic agent of qualification and emotional expression which uniquely characterizes poetry. Because of this use of rhythm, poetic statements call attention to themselves in a more emphatic way, make greater claims for the importance of their thought and feeling, dramatize more amply and more sensitively the shifting processes of emotional experience, and achieve a more subtle and complex unity of form and content than is achievable through prose. Verse is capable of more subtle suggestions of degrees of weight, significance, and emphasis, and it attains a more subtle expression of attitudes and nuances—of the process of "sentient" being of which Mrs. Langer speaks—while at the same time making possible a more flexible adjustment of emotional response to stated concept. The poet, like all users of language, has something to assert; but uniquely among them he commands an especially precise and expressive means of indicating how he feels about what he has to assert.

The well-known objections which Coleridge makes to seeing verse as the distinguishing property of a poem are easy to answer. Coleridge cites such rhymes as "Thirty days hath September" and argues that although one *may* call such compositions "poems," verses which aim at the meanly utilitarian end of facilitating memory should not be so classified. Coleridge goes on to define a "poem" as a "composition, which . . . [proposes] for its *immediate* object pleasure, not truth; . . . and [which proposes] to itself such delight from the *whole*, as is compatible with a distinct gratification from each component part."[31] He proceeds to define "poetry" in terms of the

31. *Works,* III, 371. Sidney's view coincides with Coleridge's on this issue. He says that although verse is the "fittest raiment" of poetry, verse

metaphysics of secondary imagination: poetry is that which "brings the whole soul of man into activity" by fusing idea and image, the individual and the representative, etc. Coleridge's normative definitions arbitrarily limit "poem" to those works possessing organicity of effect and "poetry" to those works which happen to embody a transcendentalist ontology. To locate the definitive feature of poetry in the nonnormative property of verse eliminates such arbitrariness. "Thirty days hath September," and other verses of this sort, cease to pose a problem: such verses are poems, all right, but they are *bad* poems or *trivial* poems, poems which do not say anything of importance and do not convey an attitude or response of any human interest.

Although any definition of a concept probably presupposes some ontological premises, it is dangerous to define poetry in terms of a particular ontology. In our period, such writers as Eliot, Yeats, Stevens, and Dylan Thomas, despite wide differences in sensibility and outlook, have shared a concern with the attempt to transcend multiplicity, fragmentation, and dissociation in experience, and their poetry often moves in the direction of affirming transcendental identities. It is not surprising that contemporary criticism, which is rooted in the poetry of its own age and to a large extent is written by the poets themselves, should tend to locate the unique essence of poetry in a peculiar way of viewing the world, or in a way of using language which implies a peculiarly poetic viewpoint—a viewpoint in which unity is sought through paradox, conflict, and contradiction. But the uniqueness of poetry cannot be successfully located in any world-view. Such poets as Jonson, Greville, Hardy, and Robinson, to name a few, do not see the world in terms of transcendental identities, and their poems

---

is "but an ornament and no cause to poetry, since there have been many most excellent poets that never versified, and now swarm many versifiers that need never answer to the name of poets." (*Defense of Poesy*, p. 11.) Sidney obviously is using "poetry" to mean literature in general. He is concerned here to define *good* poetry rather than poetry as such.

cannot be made to conform to the modern definition without misrepresentation. It is the medium of verse which uniquely characterizes poetry, not any uniquely poetic meaning which is expressed in that verse.

Conclusion

Antipropositional theorists are not, as has sometimes been charged, devotees of a cult of pure form or an art-for-art's-sake escapism. In the main, they demand that poetry be accorded a relevance to life and action, recognizing that it is only on these terms that poetry can claim any human importance. But antipropositional theory obscures and frustrates this goal of connecting the poetic and the real world. If the connection is to be established, it will be necessary to rehabilitate the concept of poetry as a mode of general statement, integrating this ancient view with the modern concept of poetry as a form of dramatic action.

For the difficulties lie not so much in the positive prescriptions about poetry of current theorists as in the unnecessarily exclusive antithesis with rational discourse out of which the prescriptions have been generated. Nothing in the foregoing critique of current theories forces us to deny that poetry is a means of organizing the emotions, that it is rich in archetypal content, that the good poem is the one which tends to involve the most inclusive synthesis of attitudes, that a poem involves a dramatization of conflicts, that poetic meaning emerges out of tensions generated by a complex verbal context. These all seem to me to be significant and valuable observations. My contention, however, is that these features of poetry cannot flourish in isolation from conceptual assertion and predication, from "opinion as to matters of fact, knowledge, belief."

Poetry and Opinion:
A Test Case

No better test case of the problem of the relationship between poetic and extrinsic standards has presented itself in the twentieth century than the controversy stimulated by the award of the Bollingen Prize of 1948 to Ezra Pound's *Pisan Cantos*. Archibald MacLeish, in a small book entitled *Poetry and Opinion*,[1] presents a concise summary of the critical issues involved, and, in attempting to free poetic criticism from considerations of ideology and commitment, comes to conclusions which are in general congenial to the poetic theories we have been examining. MacLeish's book is written in the form of a dialogue between "Mr. Saturday," who represents the opinions of the *Saturday Review of Literature* critics who attacked the decision of the Bollingen judges, and "Mr. Bollingen," who defends the award and is given the final word.

Mr. Saturday argues that the *Pisan Cantos* are marred beyond the limits of critical tolerance "because of the fascism.

1. *Poetry and Opinion* (Urbana: University of Illinois Press, 1950).

Because of the anti-Semitism. Because of the sneers at decency and the applause for murder. Because of the opinions of Mr. Pound as the poem spells his opinions out."[2] Mr. Bollingen concedes that the poem's opinions are contemptible, and he endorses T. S. Eliot's statement that the "doctrine, theory, belief, or 'view of life' presented in a poem is an integral part of the poem," but he refuses to concede that "because Mr. Pound's opinions are bad the poem must be bad."[3] He argues that the merit of a poem cannot "be judged by the merits of its political views,"[4] even when these views violate fundamental decency, and he accuses Mr. Saturday of attempting to "judge poetry from *outside* the art by external standards."[5] Mr. Saturday asks, "if . . . you really accept the opinions as an integral part of the poem—then what theory of the function of poetry will enable you to defend an award to *this* poem with *these* opinions in it?"[6] The reply is that any "justification, to be valid, must be found in the art. In the same way your condemnation of the poem because of its opinions must be a condemnation of the poem *as a poem*."[7]

The conclusion issuing from all this is that poetry indeed "is an instrument of knowledge of a certain kind—knowledge about our lives—intuitive knowledge of the kind neither reason nor science is able to supply . . ."[8] Poetry is "to reveal what exists,"[9] what the poet himself perceives.

MR. BOLLINGEN: And if what he thinks he perceives is a vast disorder; a confused, bewildered, materialistic civilization running blindly and without dignity or faith upon vulgarity and death; a generation lost to its past and its future, to

2. *Ibid.*, p. 13.
3. *Ibid.*, pp. 11, 13.
4. *Ibid.*, p. 25.
5. *Ibid.*, p. 34.
6. *Ibid.*, p. 36.
7. *Ibid.*
8. *Ibid.*, p. 43.
9. *Ibid.*

beauty and to grace;—if the coherence he perceives is this *in*-coherence, is it not precisely this his work must reveal?

MR. SATURDAY: As it is precisely this by which his work must be judged. If perception is the business of the poet then it is by the justness of his perceptions that his poems must be measured.

MR. BOLLINGEN: You seem to imply that because Pound's perception of our time and place is contemptuous of both it must lack justness. But is that true? From Baudelaire on down, poetry has thought it saw in our industrial civilization not an eternal, or even a temporal, order but a tragic disorder which made meaningless the very heart of meaning. . . . Loyalty to the art of poetry has not been synonymous, in other words, with loyalty to the society and the values it accepts.

MR. SATURDAY: But disloyalty to these values! Disloyalty to the fundamental decencies of human life! Disloyalty to human life itself![10]

Here Mr. Bollingen admits that Pound's fascism does constitute disloyalty to human life itself, but "the question is whether [its] expression here deprives the poem's insights of their meaning. . . . If it is true that poetry is an instrument of intuitive knowledge, does it not follow that the presence of opinions in a poem destroys the poem only when the opinions predetermine the intuitions—when they, and not the poet's sensibility, supply the insights?"[11] He adds that Yeats, Rimbaud, Dante, and Blake all had their opinions and theories, but that "we judge what these poets reveal to us of ourselves, not by their theories, but by our recognition of the truth of what they say—'carried alive into the heart by passion'—our passion as we read it."[12]

This distinction between opinion and sensibility prepares the way for MacLeish's vindication of the *Pisan Cantos:*

10. *Ibid.,* pp. 44–46.
11. *Ibid.,* p. 47.
12. *Ibid.,* p. 49.

. . . the poet's overriding loyalty is to his poet's conception of the world. With Pound, as this poem itself demonstrates and as the earlier Cantos make abundantly clear, the
loyalty is not to dogmas of fascism but to the poet's vision
of a tragic disorder which lies far deeper in our lives and
in our time.

MR. SATURDAY: And yet the dogma does involve the poet.
Granted that the vision of disorder is the central preoccupation—and I agree that it is—the fact that Pound himself
was attracted to fascism . . . is relevant to a judgment of
the poem. . . . How can you take his insights on faith if
he discloses himself to you, in the very act of his art, as an
adolescent or a crank or a fool who would not recognize
man's true experience if it stared him in the face?

MR. BOLLINGEN: But do the poet's opinions so disclose him
except when it is *they*, not *he*, that speak to you? Except,
that is to say, when the poet is a partisan of opinion who
serves his opinion, not his art? . . . I think the poem, with
all its evil and its ignorance about it, accomplishes in some
measure what a poem should accomplish . . . because its
poet, for all the childishness of his opinions, is loyal in the
end not to his opinions but to his art.[13]

It will be evident from this summary of the debate that Mr.
Bollingen/MacLeish relies very heavily upon the distinction
between the poet's opinions and his intuitive knowledge, and it
should be evident that this distinction will not hold up. In fact,
MacLeish arbitrarily manipulates the terms of the distinction
so as to preserve a truth content without ascribing any opinions
to the poem. MacLeish places the label "opinion" upon dogmatic mass ideologies, that is, upon opinions which he believes
to be false, and he bestows the honorific title of nonrational
"intuition" upon opinions which he regards as true. Thus
fascism is an "opinion"; the view that civilization is "a vast
disorder," etc., is an "intuition." There is really no reason why
the one set of ideas should be stigmatized as mere opinion and

13. *Ibid.*, pp. 47–51.

partisan dogma while the other is regarded as "artistic" insight
—no reason except the suspicion of abstract thought which
compels writers to construe the distinction between true and
false beliefs as a distinction between "theory" and "the facts of
experience," or between "abstractions" and "immediacies."[14] In
arguing that Pound's "contemptuous" perception of disorder
and incoherence is "just," MacLeish judges the poem in terms
of its extrapoetic opinions no less than does Mr. Saturday. He
is inconsistent in denying the relevance of standards taken
from "outside the art," unless he wishes to claim that the
incoherence of modern culture does not exist outside art.

However, the conclusion is yet to come. Mr. Saturday asks:

> So that the upshot of the whole matter is that Pound's
> poem is good in spite of its evil. . . .
> MR. BOLLINGEN: Not in spite of its evil: including its evil. It
> is only with its evil about it that this poem can give this
> poet's vision of hell. For he himself is damned in it and
> speaks.
> MR. SATURDAY: So that the upshot of the whole matter is
> this: that we are to regard the judges in this case as
> justified because our time expects so little of the art they
> judged!
> MR. BOLLINGEN: Is it so little to ask of any art, even the
> greatest, that it give mankind, in such an age as ours, an
> image of our lives?[15]

The argumentative strategy has been suddenly reversed. Previously, the fascistic and anti-Semitic opinions were seen as
extrapoetic elements which could be ignored since the poem
contained more important revelations, "intuitions" which constituted the *real* poetry. Now, however, the virulent opinions
are given a positive justification in terms of a principle of
dramatic propriety. In a poem which deals with and is ad-

14. Of course it is true that highly programmatic statements of
ideology are likely to serve poorly as material for poetry, but this is a
limitation of certain kinds of opinions, not of opinions as such.
15. *Poetry and Opinion*, pp. 51–52.

dressed to an evil and decaying civilization it is appropriate that the narrator be "himself damned" and in hell, and thus it is right for him to indulge in inhumane and vicious doctrines. Presumably, if MacLeish's argument is taken seriously, the poem is all the better for its racist statements. We should be pleased that they are there, since the more racist and the more inhumane they are, the more effectively will the horrifying "image of our lives" be driven home.

As a strategy for rescuing intellectually unacceptable poetry, this attempt to transform base intellectual metal into poetic gold seems even more desperate and arbitrary than the distinction between opinion and intuition. For one thing, MacLeish's effort to see Pound's opinions as dramatically justified forces him to impose an interpretation upon the poem that it cannot bear. MacLeish ignores the fact that when Pound gives vent to his opinions his point of view is not one of awareness of the evil of his position, but rather one of self-righteous conviction of the truth and virtue of what he is saying. By taking the inhumane statements as dramatic confirmation of the hell and evil which the poem says we all share, MacLeish is bringing to the poem an attitude of self-condemnation which does not appear in it. When Pound writes:

> the yidd is a stimulant, and the goyim are cattle
> in gt/proportion and go to saleable slaughter
> with the maxium of docility . . .[16]

he advances his idea in all earnestness, and we cannot read it as the self-condemnation of a soul aware that it is suffering in hell without adding a humane perspective to the statement which it does not contain.

But the significant point for the present discussion is that MacLeish is here not so much begging the question of belief in poetry as providing support for the position he wishes to oppose. For he is converting Pound's actual opinion, which he

16. *The Cantos (1–95)* (New York: New Directions, 1956), Canto LXXIV, p. 17.

cannot share, into an ironic counteropinion which he can: he is converting the poem's meaning into something to which he can assent: that modern men are possessed by evil, damned to a hell of hatred of their fellows and love of destruction. Again, as with the resort to "intuitive knowledge," MacLeish *pretends* to vindicate the poem on nonideological, purely artistic grounds but in fact smuggles in belief criteria under the counter.

I am ready to accept MacLeish's argument that Pound's poem is not wholly contaminated by its fascist ideology, that the vision of the disintegration of contemporary civilization is powerfully conveyed, that many passages achieve greatness:

> The ant's a centaur in his dragon world.
> Pull down thy vanity, it is not man
> Made courage, or made order, or made grace,
>   Pull down thy vanity, I say pull down.
> Learn of the green world what can be thy place
> In scaled invention or true artistry,
> Pull down thy vanity,
>   Paquin pull down!
> The green casque has outdone your elegance.[17]

These lines, which MacLeish quotes, are justly celebrated, but we should admit that they are no less abstract and "ideological" than those parts of the poem which deal explicitly with social credit or Jews.

On the other hand, MacLeish has not provided a good answer to Mr. Saturday's question: "How can you take his insights on faith if he discloses himself to you, in the very act of his art, as an adolescent or a crank or a fool who would not recognize man's true experience if it stared him in the face?" It does no good to reply that this is only "the poet's opinions" speaking, not the poetry itself, for the opinions and the attitudes they inspire are *in* the poetry and cannot be arbitrarily separated from it. The poem often rises to a tone of elevation

17. *Ibid.*, Canto LXXXI, p. 99.

and seriousness and invites the reader to share its emotion. If the emotion comes across as rooted in an adolescent or crank point of view, then the attitude will be to that extent impossible for the reader to identify himself with imaginatively, and the poem will fail for him. Though passages of Pound's poem can be exempted from this criticism, large portions of it cannot be; the poem simply goes too far in violating what M. H. Abrams calls "the beliefs and prepossessions of our common experience, common sense, and common moral consciousness."[18] This is an "extrinsic" judgment, to be sure, but that does not mean it is not a *poetic* and *artistic* judgment. Because the ideas and human attitudes are an intrinsic part of the poem, to judge the poem as a poem is also to judge it as a human act, and that judgment cannot be separated from considerations of intellectual soundness.

18. *Literature and Belief*, English Institute Essays, 1957, ed. M. H. Abrams (New York: Columbia University Press, 1958), p. 28.

"*The Poet Nothing Affirmeth*"

It may be instructive to note the frequency with which Sidney's general theory of poetry has been interpreted by contemporary poetic theorists in terms of one of the antithetical poles of the statement-drama opposition. On the one hand, there is the view represented by Murray Krieger, who accuses Sidney of viewing poetic discourse as the mere sugar-coating or decoration of a propositional pill.[1] On the other side are those who see in the famous remark that the poet "nothing affirmeth, and therefore never lieth" a remarkable anticipation of modern antipropositionalist theory:

> Through the Pléiade to Sidney there ran the argument that poets were not competent to make philosophical statements; they affirm nothing (Frank Kermode).[2]

1. *The New Apologists for Poetry* (Minneapolis: University of Minnesota Press, 1956), pp. 171–72.
2. "The Argument of Marvell's Garden," *Seventeenth Century Poetry*, ed. William R. Keast (New York: Oxford University Press, 1962), p. 304, n. 4.

Poetry is truth of "coherence," rather than truth of "correspondence," as the matter is sometimes phrased nowadays. We have heard Sir Philip Sidney say that the poet nothing affirmeth and therefore never lieth (W. K. Wimsatt).[3]

"A poem should not mean but be." It is an epigram worth quoting in every essay on poetry. And the poet "nothing affirmeth and therefore never lieth" (Wimsatt).[4]

In all literary verbal structures the final direction of meaning is inward. In literature the standards of outward meaning are secondary, for literary works do not pretend to describe or assert, and hence are not true, not false, and yet not tautological either. . . . As Sir Philip Sidney remarked, "the poet never affirmeth," and therefore does not lie any more than he tells the truth (Frye).[5]

Far from being taken as sterile didacticism, in these passages Sidney's view is celebrated as an expression of the same order and import as "a poem should not mean but be."

The contemporary critical tendency to view the problem of poetic meaning in terms of the mutually exclusive alternatives of *either* statement *or* enactment seems to have blinded these critics to the synthetic aspects of the classical theory which Sidney's *Defense* restates. Nothing could be more far-fetched than to read the remark that the poet "nothing affirmeth, and therefore never lieth" as if it meant that poets are "not competent to make philosophical statements." Such a denial would have dismayed Sidney, who emphasizes the philosophical importance of poetry and points out that poets were the world's first philosophers.

In context, Sidney's famous disclaimer comes as a rebuttal to the literalistic objection that the fictions of poetry are deceit-

---

3. *Literary Criticism: A Short History* (New York: Random House, 1957), p. 748.
4. *The Verbal Icon* (Lexington: University of Kentucky Press, 1954), p. 81.
5. *Anatomy of Criticism* (Princeton, N. J.: Princeton University Press, 1957), pp. 74–76.

ful, the same misconception which Dr. Johnson was to demol-
ish conclusively in the *Preface to Shakespeare*. Sidney asks,
"What child is there that, coming to a play, and seeing Thebes
written in great letters upon an old door, doth believe that it is
Thebes?"[6] When Sidney says that the poet affirms nothing, he
means only to point out that poets do not claim to represent
the actual, historical Thebes on the stage and that the audience
does not expect them to. The poet is not responsible for the
sort of accuracy to fact which binds the historian.

Throughout the *Defense,* Sidney clearly indicates that the
poet affirms general philosophic truth. M. H. Abrams writes:

> According to [Sidney's] logic of poetic statements . . . the
> poet embodies a true "generall notion" in an invented "par-
> ticular example," and so, under the transparent guise of
> making declarative historical assertions, actually poses to the
> reader an implicit optative or imperative—the poet "not
> labouring to tell you what is, or is not, but what should or
> should not be."[7]

Although this allegorical conception of poetic truth may be
liable to Krieger's indictment as a decoration theory, this tendency of his theory is checked by his statement that the poet's
style must be in due proportion to the "dignity of the subject."[8] In this statement, as we have seen, Sidney not only
declares the obligation of the poet to speak the truth, to
represent the subject in its true "dignity," but specifies a vital
connection between that truth and the poet's manner of writing.

Although Sidney's conception of poetic truth is grounded in
a transcendental Neo-Platonism, his view harmonizes with the
ancient conception of truth as an affair of rationality. Plato had
made philosophical dialectic the prime means of arriving at the

6. *The Defense of Poesy*, ed. Albert S. Cook (Boston: Ginn and Co.,
1890), p. 36.
7. *The Mirror and the Lamp: Romantic Theory and the Critical
Tradition* (New York: Oxford University Press, 1953), p. 323.
8. *Defense of Poesy*, p. 11.

realm of Ideas; in later antiquity, art is entered into competition with dialectic as a means of reaching the Ideas by theorists who do not set art in opposition to rational thought but who see art as combining reason with the concrete phenomena of the senses. Poetic emotions are thus firmly grounded in a rational, cognitive order of knowledge, and are bound to this order by the principle of decorum.[9]

Abrams describes the way in which the Neo-Platonic concept of the Idea received a subjectivist turn in romantic theory: "Both in the Renaissance and later, Platonist aesthetics . . . customarily located the Ideas both within and without the mind" and thus "guaranteed the impersonality of the artist's vision by making metaphysical provision for linking the Idea in the individual mind to the universal and unchanging Ideas of the world-pattern." When the Idea is sought by "turning the eye of the mind inward," as when "the work is conceived to imitate something inside the artist himself," then "art readily slips its moorings in the public world of sense experience and begins to rely instead on a vision which is personal and subjective."[10] In antiquity and through the Renaissance, the artistic idea, however transcendentally it is conceived, is subject to verification by experience according to the laws of rational understanding, conditions which no longer apply in the romantic theory of creative imagination. Thus Sidney can proclaim the poet's freedom to range freely "within the zodiac of his own wit"[11] without really subscribing to Northrop Frye's theory of the autonomy of the imagination, since for Sidney the poet is always accountable to the ultimate laws of experience, what he calls "the general reason of things."[12] Whatever the legitimacy of the theory of imaginative autonomy and the nonpropositional nature of poetry, its proponents cannot properly claim Sidney as an ally.

9. See Erwin Panofsky, *Idea: A Concept in Art Theory* (Columbia, S. C.: University of South Carolina Press, 1968), pp. 51–52.
10. *Mirror and the Lamp*, p. 43.
11. *Defense of Poesy*, p. 7.
12. *Ibid.*, p. 15.

Index

Index